WILLIAM WOR
POETRY

Continuum *Reader's Guides*

Continuum *Reader's Guides* are clear, concise and accessible introductions to classic literary texts. Each book explores the themes, context, criticism and influence of key works, providing a practical introduction to close reading and guiding the reader towards a thorough understanding of the text. Ideal for undergraduate students, the guides provide an essential resource for anyone who needs to get to grips with a literary text.

WILLIAM WORDSWORTH'S POETRY

A Reader's Guide

DANIEL ROBINSON

continuum

Continuum International Publishing Group

The Tower Building	80 Maiden Lane
11 York Road	Suite 704
London SE1 7NX	New York, NY 10038

www.continuumbooks.com

British Library Cataloguing-in-Publication Data
A catalogue record for this book is available from the British Library.

ISBN: 978-1-4411-8395-8 (hardcover)
978-1-4411-4587-1 (paperback)

Library of Congress Cataloging-in-Publication Data
Robinson, Daniel, 1969-
William Wordsworth's poetry / Daniel Robinson.
p. cm. – (Reader's guides)
Includes index.
ISBN: 978-1-4411-8395-8 (hardcover)
ISBN: 978-1-4411-4587-1 (pbk.)
1. Wordsworth, William, 1770-1850–Criticism and interpretation.
I. Title. II. Series.

PR5888.R55 2010
821'.7–dc22

2010000466

Typeset by Newgen Imaging Systems Pvt Ltd, Chennai, India
Printed and bound in Great Britain by the MPG Books Group

*Every great Poet is a Teacher: I wish either
to be considered as a Teacher, or as nothing.*

—William Wordsworth,
letter to Sir George Beaumont,
February 1808
(*Middle Years* 1.195)

CONTENTS

NOTE ON EDITIONS

For material from and related to *Lyrical Ballads* I refer to the following source, abbreviated in parenthetical citations as *LBRW*:

Richey, William, and Daniel Robinson, eds. *Lyrical Ballads and Related Writings*. (New Riverside Edition) Boston: Houghton Mifflin, 2002.

For the texts of Wordsworth's poetry other than the 1798 *Lyrical Ballads* I quote from and refer to Stephen Gill's *Major Works*, abbreviated as *MW*:

Gill, Stephen, ed. *William Wordsworth: The Major Works*. (Oxford World's Classics) 1984. Oxford: Oxford UP, 2008.

ACKNOWLEDGMENTS

As always, I am grateful for the love and support of my family, Wendy Warren and Sarah Margaret Robinson. In particular, I would like to thank members of the Wordsworth reading group I conducted in the summer of 2009. These participants helped me immensely as I worked on this book: Nicole DeGuio, Melissa Lucchesi, Samantha Marker, Sara-Jane Rice, and Allison Roelofs. I would like to thank my dean, Matthew Poslusny, for assistance and support during the completion of this project.

Special thanks go to my colleague and friend Janine Utell, who graciously read and commented upon the book.

This book bears the influence of many teachers, scholars, and colleagues; but I am especially grateful for the friendship of and collaboration with Bill Richey (1956–2003), who shared my enthusiasm for Wordsworth and who greatly informed my thinking about Wordsworth's poetry.

CHAPTER 1

CONTEXTS

In his popular study of *Genius*, literary critic Harold Bloom, who began his career as a specialist in Romantic poetry, makes an undeniable claim: 'After Wordsworth poets are Wordsworthian whether they know it—as Shelley, Keats, Tennyson, Frost did—or not' (377). Even writers who may not seem Wordsworthian—such as Byron, Robert Browning, Wilde, T. S. Eliot, Stevens—nonetheless had to define themselves in relation or in opposition to what it means to be Wordsworthian. What it means to be Wordsworthian is the subject of this book. And I start with Bloom's comment because it reflects a fundamental truth of what most people think about poetry. Bloom's point is that Wordsworth is the 'inventor' of poetry that replaces 'subject-matter [with] the poet's subjectivity' (377). For better, in the case of good poets, or worse, in the case of bad ones, Wordsworth's legacy is the general understanding that poetry is about the subjective expression of any poet's peculiar view of the world. This is why readers today find it difficult to think of long narrative poems such as *The Odyssey* or *Paradise Lost* as poetry. The influence of Wordsworth on our culture has instilled the idea of poetry as an outlet for the personal expression of feeling. And he gave us what has now become the caricature of poets as sensitive, solitary naturalists wandering lonely as clouds. Or to put it another way, Wordsworth's poetic legacy is the permanent privileging of the lyric mode. Along with this result is his insistence on simpler, more conversational language—his banishment of 'flowery' diction. He is therefore *the* English poet to have had the greatest impact on literary history after Milton; in terms of a popular conception of poetry, he is undoubtedly more important than Milton. Simply put, poetry after Wordsworth is more recognizable as poetry to today's reader than what comes before Wordsworth.

Wordsworth epitomizes Romanticism: William Hazlitt wrote that 'Mr Wordsworth's genius is a pure emanation of the Spirit of the Age' (161). For a time, what we now call the Romantic period was known as 'the Age of Wordsworth.' He lived longer than any of the other five major Romantics (Blake, Coleridge, Byron, Shelley, Keats), three of whom are famous for having died young. Born in 1770 (the same year as Beethoven), Wordsworth, in contrast to the other Romantics, lived to be 80; by then he had become a fixture of Victorian literature, serving for the last seven years of his life as the Queen's Poet Laureate. He was succeeded in that position upon his death in 1850 by Tennyson, whose *In Memoriam A. H. H.* appeared in the same year. The span of Wordsworth's life is remarkable for its longevity and for his productivity but also for the major upheavals in politics, society, and aesthetics that took place during it-most notably the American War for Independence, the French Revolution and Napoleonic Wars, the ongoing Enlightenment, the rise of the working class and the Industrial Revolution, the expansion of reading audiences and the growth of publishing, and the literary and artistic moment/movement that we now call 'Romanticism.' Although periodization is at times a vexed issue (see Chapter 5), Wordsworth stands both at the forefront of Romanticism and in the midst of the aesthetic transition from eighteenth-century tastes and ideas to nineteenth-century ones much in the same way that Beethoven does in music, that Kant does in philosophy, and that Goya and Constable do in painting. Although he is firmly established today as the pre-eminent Romantic poet, Wordsworth, like many who challenge convention, had to endure considerable critical ridicule, public neglect, and financial insecurity before he finally enjoyed success in his later years.

EARLY LIFE

Wordsworth was born on April 7, 1770 in Cockermouth, a small town near the northwest coast of England, in the Lake District, one of England's most literary regions, having also been home to Robert Southey, Samuel Taylor Coleridge, John Ruskin, and Beatrix Potter. The Lake District famously is also the setting of much of Wordsworth's poetry. His father was a well-to-do lawyer who represented the powerful and influential Sir James

Lowther, later the first Lord Lonsdale. His sister, Dorothy, who would be Wordsworth's companion for most of their lives, was born in 1771 and was baptized with him. They had one older brother, Richard, and two younger brothers, John and Christopher. The Wordsworth children lived and played happily together, Wordsworth in particular enjoying the experience of growing up in the country and on the banks of the river Derwent. As the first two books of his autobiographical poem *The Prelude* show, no influence is more essential to Wordsworth's poetry than his childhood experiences in nature. Upon the death of their mother, however, in 1778, six-year-old Dorothy was sent to live with relatives and would not see her brother William for almost a decade. Wordsworth, the following year, entered Hawkshead Grammar School, one of England's finest, thus marking him for matriculation at Cambridge. At Hawkshead the young Wordsworth studied classical literature as well as Milton and Shakespeare, but he also read widely in contemporary authors such as James Thomson, Robert Burns, Charlotte Smith, Oliver Goldsmith, and George Crabbe. In 1787 his first published poem, 'Sonnet on Seeing Miss Helen Maria Williams Weep at a Tale of Distress,' appeared in the *European Magazine* under the pseudonym 'Axiologus,' which literally means 'Wordsworth.' The sonnet is a response to Williams's epic poem *Peru* (1784), a critique of European colonialism in South America. Later that year, he began his undistinguished four-year period of study at St. John's College, Cambridge, during which time he abandoned his tentative intention to become a clergyman but continued to read books and write poetry.

DOROTHY WORDSWORTH

'She gave me eyes, she gave me ears': so Wordsworth writes of his sister's influence on him in the poem 'The Sparrow's Nest' (1807). Wordsworth's reunion with Dorothy as an adult is one of the more significant moments in his life. He addressed his first major publication, *An Evening Walk*, to her in 1793, and she is a crucial presence in *Lyrical Ballads*, particularly in 'Lines Written at a Small Distance from My House' and 'Tintern Abbey.' She was with him for almost all of his personal and professional trials and successes. And she was in some ways his collaborator, having had an exceptional education for a young woman of the eighteenth century. After their childhood separation, William and Dorothy lived together from 1795 until his death. She was present, perhaps even actively involved, when Wordsworth and Coleridge conceived *Lyrical Ballads* in Somerset; she journeyed with them to Germany and set up residence with her brother at Grasmere in 1799. Dorothy remained an integral part of the family after Wordsworth married Mary Hutchinson in 1802. And she was a writer too: although she composed poetry and travel-writing, she is most famous for *The Grasmere Journal*, which she began writing in order to 'give Wm Pleasure' (1) but also to preserve details of people and places that he could use for his poetry. In addition to much information about their daily lives, she records meeting the Leech-Gatherer ('Resolution and Independence'), seeing the dancing daffodils ('I Wandered Lonely as a Cloud'), crossing Westminster Bridge in the morning (the sonnet 'Composed upon Westminster Bridge'), and observing her brother hard at work on 'the poem to Coleridge' (*The Prelude*). Her writing, however, has its own vitality and passion and it shows a woman deeply and actively involved in the construction and maintenance not only of Wordsworth's household but also of his poetic identity. Like Keats's letters, her journals offer another, more private, though no less fascinating, genre of Romantic-period writing. Dorothy Wordsworth's importance in the process of her brother's composition continues to be a fruitful subject of study, particularly after the influence of feminist criticism and, more pertinent to Wordsworth studies *per se*, the advent of historical approaches and advances in the textual study of Wordsworth's manuscripts.

WORDSWORTH IN THE 1790s

The 1790s are formative years in Wordsworth's intellectual development; they were tumultuous years for anyone living in England and through the political and cultural upheaval that was the French Revolution. This decade in Wordsworth's career, therefore, is particularly interesting because of his responses to his world at the turn of the century and because it culminates with the first and second editions of *Lyrical Ballads*. Looking for Wordsworth during the 1790s we find him figuring out what as a poet he wanted to say, whereas in the first decade of the nineteenth century and thereafter we find him working on what kind of poet he wanted to *be*.

Upon completing his B.A. at Cambridge, Wordsworth tasted youthful political exuberance on the streets of Paris, during his first visit to France and Switzerland in 1790. In *The Prelude*, Wordsworth famously writes, 'Bliss was it in that dawn to be alive, / But to be young was very heaven!' (10.692–3). The excitement of the revolutionaries was infectious and matched for Wordsworth the sublime experience of crossing the Alps during the same trip. After a year back in London, Wordsworth returned to France more interested in political affairs and became friends with the French general and revolutionary Michel Beaupuy, who inspired Wordsworth with the belief 'that a spirit was abroad / Which could not be withstood' (*Prelude* 9.521–2). As he became increasingly committed to the cause of liberty, he also had a love affair with a French woman named Annette Vallon, who subsequently became pregnant; Wordsworth, finding himself in need of means to support a family, returned to England. But the outbreak of war between England and France prevented his return and initiated both a personal and political crisis that took a great emotional toll on him. His loyalty to the cause of liberty painfully conflicted with his love of country. He found himself wandering aimlessly through England and into Wales, where he first visited Tintern Abbey, the setting of one of his most famous poems.

During the first half of the 1790s Wordsworth supported the principles of the French Revolution, calling himself a democrat and describing himself as an opponent of aristocracy, hereditary privilege, and even the British constitutional monarchy (*Early Years* 119, 123–4). In London, Wordsworth associated with radical intellectuals, began working on a protest poem of sorts called 'Salisbury Plain,' and even considered participating in the pamphlet war that arose from debate over the French Revolution. In 1793, Richard Watson, Bishop of Llandaff, publicly disavowed the French Revolution, after initially supporting it; like many British liberals, Watson could no longer stomach revolutionary violence, particularly as it reached its nadir in the execution of King Louis XVI and the subsequent Reign of Terror. Wordsworth later would feel the same way, but in 1793 he wrote an angry

'Letter to the Bishop of Llandaff' (which did not appear in print until 1876). Although the Paine-influenced pamphlet was never published, it survives as a document of the young Wordsworth's enthusiasm for the cause of 'true Liberty,' his call for manhood suffrage, his championing of working-class values, and his distaste for aristocratic privilege. He held out hope throughout Robespierre's reign that the course of the Revolution would be righted. Of course, in a few years—and only a couple of hundred lines later in *The Prelude*—Wordsworth would come to see the terrible irony of the Revolution's having executed a king only 'to crown an Emperor'; Wordsworth bitterly compares the French people's embracing of Napoleon to a 'dog / Returning to its vomit' (10.933–4).

Despite the violence in France, radical and liberal Britons alike saw the Revolution as an opportunity to gauge the efficacy of their own government and the 'Glorious Revolution' of 1688, in comparison with the perceived advancements of democracy in both the newly independent American states and in the French *Déclaration des droits de l'Homme et du citoyen*. Edmund Burke's *Reflections on the Revolution in France* (1790) expressed concern that revolutionary sentiments might spread to England and other European countries. Skeptical of capitalism and the bourgeoisie, the French Third Estate, Burke warned against revolution, predicted chaos in France, and asserted the validity of Britain's class structure and the value of religious and social traditions. Burke famously was rebutted by Mary Wollstonecraft in her *Vindication of the Rights of Men* (1790) and by Thomas Paine in his *Rights of Man* (1791–1792); both attack Burke for his defense of hierarchy, and defend the Revolution and its correspondent democratic values. Well aware of the continuing debate, Wordsworth particularly was influenced by William Godwin's more philosophical and less overtly polemical treatise *An Enquiry Concerning the Principles of Political Justice* (1793). As the British government seemed bent on restoring monarchical rule to France while attempting to suppress what it deemed sedition at home, Godwin's book, which was no less critical of aristocracy, managed to speak to liberal intellectuals disenchanted with the Revolution by advocating 'the still and quiet progress of reason' instead of violent disruptive upheaval (Godwin 1: 204). Basically Godwin believed in the infinite progress of humankind through the perfection of reason and virtue, suggesting a path to egalitarian principles free of violent passions such as those that seemed to be driving the Revolution after 1792. After Wordsworth's experiences in France and with French politics, Godwin's utilitarian rationalism, his ideas about the 'perfectibility of man,' and his rejection of violence appealed to a young man searching for ballast.

Turning away from foreign politics toward conditions at home, Wordsworth became increasingly aware of the plight of the rural poor, which was especially dire by the mid-1790s due to poor harvests and rising food prices, and which would become a significant subject for his poetry. He embraced Godwin's notions about benevolence and philanthropy and shared Godwin's belief that society creates its own criminals through inequality. Godwin believed that society could function only if people do the right things because they care about one another, and that government, laws, and punishment never will make people truly good. Inspired by Godwin, Wordsworth even planned to publish a political journal called *The Philanthropist*. But it was Godwin's utilitarianism that seemed impervious to compassion and ultimately left Wordsworth cold. By the time Wordsworth wrote his play *The Borderers* in 1796, he had come to find Godwin's reason incompatible with feeling, and he makes Godwinian reason a theme in the play and the source of its tragedy. Godwin's philosophy was for him insufficient as a means of perfecting humankind because Wordsworth believed in the fundamentally irrational elements of the human psyche that include kindness, hope, sympathy, faith, and love.

Wordsworth became a poet in this political environment and developed a social vision from it. Although he is often reckoned a poet of nature, Wordsworth thought of himself as a poet of humankind. As we shall see, in most of Wordsworth's poetry the poet shows how the love of nature can have a morally redemptive effect and thus lead to the love of humankind, what Aristotle calls *philia*. Many readers over the past two centuries have mistaken the Wordsworthian solitary as a rejection of humankind—Shelley's poem 'Alastor; or the Spirit of Solitude,' for example, reads Wordsworth this way. But when reading Wordsworth, one should always consider how what he is representing in verse may have a larger impact on society—or at least the potential impact he may have intended it to have. Wordsworth's poetry is always about society and his relationship to its members, even though it may seem to be removed from the world. The Wordsworthian figure may escape society for moral and spiritual renovation; but, like Plato's philosopher, he must go back into the cave and instruct the others. The great ambition of his life—never achieved—was to write *The Recluse*, conceived as 'a philosophical Poem, containing views of Man, Nature, and Society' (Preface to *The Excursion* [1814] viii). The best way to read Wordsworth, then, is to look for the ways in which the complexity of diction and figure, of representation itself, works against overly simplistic interpretations or overly determined assertions, revealing a poetic imagination deeply involved in 'the essential passions of the heart' and profoundly committed to the 'native and naked dignity of man.' Wordsworth described a poet as 'the rock of defence of human nature; an upholder and preserver, carrying every where with him relationship and love' (*LBRW* 402). It is fitting, then, that he would realize his vocation as a poet in reunion with his sister and in collaboration with a friend.

COLERIDGE

By 1795, the intellectual circle of radicals and reformers in which Wordsworth found himself soon brought him into contact with journalist, poet, and lecturer Samuel Taylor Coleridge, who shared an interest in radical politics and in Godwin's philosophy, although Coleridge's religious orientation made him more quickly suspicious of Godwin's rationalism than Wordsworth was. Already the more established writer of the two, Coleridge had a dazzling intellect that showed itself most brilliantly in conversation, and his learned discourse provided Wordsworth with new material for philosophical contemplation. Just as his faith in Godwin was waning, Wordsworth inherited £900, a large sum of money, upon the death of a friend for whom he had cared during illness. The money enabled him to live independently, with Dorothy as his companion, at Racedown Lodge in Dorset. The relative isolation there gave Wordsworth a much-needed respite from urban politics and an opportunity to resume poetry. His relationship with Coleridge, who was living nearby at Bristol, advanced to the point of sending poems in

8

manuscript for Coleridge's review, and Wordsworth mixed with Coleridge's literary friends Charles Lamb and Robert Southey. The admiration between the two men was mutual: Coleridge proclaimed Wordsworth 'the best poet of the age' and 'a great man' (*Letters* 1: 215, 327). In *The Prelude* Wordsworth acknowledges Coleridge's importance after he 'Yielded up moral questions in despair': 'Thou, most precious Friend! about this time / First known to me, didst lend a living help / To regulate my Soul' (10.900, 905–7). Much of Wordsworth's future success and some of his failure is attributable to Coleridge's powerful influence. Coleridge made Wordsworth think more consciously about the importance of having literary principles as the foundation for poetry, an important step in shaping Wordsworth's poetic identity. And later it was Coleridge who inspired Wordsworth's most ambitious project, *The Recluse*, the epic poem that Coleridge urged his friend to write in order to establish himself as the first major poet since Milton. It was to be a greater *Paradise Regained*, grounded in philosophy, nature, spirituality, and humanity—a work that would revivify a dispirited age and renovate humankind. At least that was the plan. Wordsworth began in 1799 the poem that would become *The Prelude*, so called because Wordsworth conceived of it as the 'ante-chamber' to the philosophical poem that Coleridge had implored him to write. Coleridge believed that 'Wordsworth possessed more of the genius of a great philosophic poet than any man I ever knew, or, as I believe, has existed in England since Milton; but it seems to me that he ought never to have abandoned the contemplative position which is peculiarly—perhaps I might say exclusively— fitted for him' (*Specimens* 2: 71–2). Coleridge went to his grave disappointed that Wordsworth never followed the path for which Coleridge felt he was destined—that of a philosopher-poet. *The Prelude*, however, would turn out to be Wordsworth's masterpiece—and Wordsworth himself referred to it primarily as 'the poem to Coleridge.'

In 1797 Coleridge arranged for Wordsworth and his sister to rent Alfoxden House, near Nether Stowey, where Coleridge and his family resided. The four-mile walk almost daily over the Quantock hills gave rise to their famous collaboration, the 1798 volume *Lyrical Ballads; with a Few Other Poems*. Their talks concentrated on what Coleridge described later in his *Biographia*

Literaria as 'the poetry of nature.' Together, they distinguished 'two cardinal points of poetry'—sympathy and imagination—and began work on a poem they hoped would earn some money. Upon Wordsworth's suggestion of a sailor who kills an albatross, Coleridge began writing 'The Rime of the Ancyent Marinere,' as the idea for the *Lyrical Ballads* volume began to take shape. According to Coleridge, Wordsworth's poems were subjects 'chosen from ordinary life,' while Coleridge's were about 'incidents and agents . . . in part at least supernatural' (*Biographia* 2: 5–6). Although they cowrote only one or two poems, their collaboration involved what Thomas McFarland calls 'symbiosis' or what Paul Magnuson calls 'lyrical dialogue.' In general, Coleridge had a more obvious influence on Wordsworth's poetry, while Coleridge's sense of inferiority to Wordsworth hindered his own poetic projects: he simply felt he was not as good a poet as Wordsworth was. Years later in his *Biographia Literaria*, Coleridge would criticize Wordsworth's explanation of the poetic principles behind *Lyrical Ballads*, while also defending Wordsworth's poetic talents (see Chapter 4). As Lucy Newlyn has shown, Wordsworth's greatest work, *The Prelude*, while in some ways a tribute, is also a reaction against Coleridge's influence. Even after it ended in practice, the collaboration continued in spirit. Wordsworth and Coleridge would be a presence in each other's work as long as they both lived.

THE ENLIGHTENMENT: SENSE AND SENSIBILITY

One of the caricatures of the Romantic poets is that they were emotionally overwrought—and they may seem so compared with the ostensibly more cerebral Milton or Pope—but they too were intellectually rigorous and contributed to the intellectual history of the Enlightenment. I prefer to see Romanticism as part of the development of the Enlightenment rather than a reaction against it. While poet-artist William Blake at times appears to be whole-heartedly opposed to Enlightenment ideals of reason, personified in his work by empiricists John Locke and Sir Isaac Newton, Wordsworth and Coleridge were profoundly interested in eighteenth-century ideas about epistemology, perception, and feeling. Although the Enlightenment in its eighteenth-century incarnation is called 'the Age of Reason,' writers and philosophers of the period were interested in both thinking and feeling—a presumed polarity that Jane Austen plays upon for the title of her end-of-the-century novel *Sense and Sensibility* (1811). While 'sense' is grounded in reason, 'sensibility' as a concept in the eighteenth century referred to the capacity to feel and experience emotion. The empiricists' emphasis on sense-perception as the primary source of knowledge paradoxically gave rise to a popular aesthetic of sensibility, a taste for art that affects the emotions. Even the great Scottish empiricist David Hume attributed moral thinking to feeling, and his fellow Scot Adam Smith, in his *Theory of Moral Sentiments* (1759), argued that sympathy is essential to moral development and is an important element in the appreciation of literature. Along the same lines, and significantly in the same year as the first edition of *Lyrical Ballads*, 1798, playwright Joanna Baillie wrote that it is the 'sympathetic curiosity of our nature' to which all great literature appeals. The belief that art should arouse sympathy led to the popularity of literature of sensibility, which includes novels such as Henry Mackenzie's *Man of Feeling* (1771) and Goethe's *Sorrows of Young Werther* (1774), as well as poetry by such popular authors as Joseph Warton, William Collins, William Cowper, Helen Maria Williams, Charlotte Smith, Erasmus Darwin, and William Lisle Bowles—all of whom influenced Wordsworth and Coleridge. These works of extreme emotionalism provided a popular version of Locke's ideas about how all knowledge comes from experience, or more specifically from the senses; and of the emphasis on sympathy in the philosophy of Smith as well as Swiss philosopher Jean-Jacques Rousseau. But sensibility, or the ability to feel great emotion, taken to extremes, as Austen's novel warns, can be dangerous—especially for young women who allow their feelings to control them.

Like Austen, Wordsworth and Coleridge believed that literature ought to involve the head and the heart in equal measure—and should inspire feelings of pity and compassion. But Wordsworth is concerned that stories of others' misery not be consumed for entertainment, as we shall see in Chapter 3; thus his pedlar character in 'The Ruined Cottage' (about which more in that upcoming chapter) remarks in midst of narrating a story of suffering,

It were a wantonness and would demand
Severe reproof, if we were men whose hearts

Could hold vain dalliance with the misery
Even of the dead, contented thence to draw
A momentary pleasure never marked
By reason, barren of all future good. (221–6)

The pleasures of popular culture, such as literature of sensibility then or sad songs and movies today, frequently include a shallow sentimentality that pulls on the heartstrings but provides no lasting effect, much less a serious involvement in the actual misery of real people. Adam Smith's *Theory of Moral Sentiments* placed great importance on the role of imagination in sympathy and thus created an environment in which literature of sensibility could evolve into the kind of humanitarian poetry Wordsworth and Coleridge would write. Wordsworth particularly becomes increasingly interested in the possibility of 'future good' resulting from the combination of reason and emotion. Wordsworth famously wrote that 'all good poetry is the spontaneous overflow of powerful feeling'—a phrase often quoted out of context to give the impression that Wordsworth is advocating poetry as effusion. But 'spontaneous' in the eighteenth century meant not unpremeditated or impulsive, but voluntary. So Wordsworth does not mean that poetry is the result of some accidental surge of emotion; rather, the poet wills that great emotion should inform the process of composition. He does so with a distinct purpose beyond what we might think of as self-expression or writing-as-therapy. Good poetry, according to Wordsworth, is written by poets who possess 'more than usual organic sensibility'—and here he uses 'sensibility' to denote a more strictly Lockean ability to perceive and to experience. As he explains further in his 1815 Preface, good poets have a wider range of perceptions (*MW* 626). Yet he also asserts that all good poems have been composed by poets who have 'thought long and deeply.' For Wordsworth, as he writes elsewhere, 'the excellence of writing . . . consists in a conjunction of Reason and Passion,' adding, straight out of the Enlightenment discussion, that this 'conjunction' 'must be of necessity benign' because 'the taste, intellectual power and morals of a country are inseparably linked in mutual dependence' (*Prose* 2: 85). Taste becomes an important element of Wordsworth's understanding of himself as a poet—particularly within a culture that rapidly was changing and seemingly was advancing. A more literate population as well as continued advances in printing gave rise to the publishing industry and the popularity of prose fiction. But the democratization of literature did not guarantee an improvement in taste—quite the contrary.

Enlightenment thinking emphasizes the progressive power of the human mind to understand the universe, but some thinkers, such as Rousseau, doubted that human society was progressing along a path of infinite perfectibility. Rousseau even argued that advances in the arts and sciences, and thus in society more broadly, were corrupting humankind. Moreover, Wordsworth and Coleridge came to understand some of the same limitations to the two main strands of Enlightenment thought—empiricism and rationalism—that Hume and Immanuel Kant did. Empiricists believe that knowledge comes from the acquisition of experience, while rationalists believe that knowledge comes a priori from the exercise of reason. Kant believed that neither approach could lead to a complete understanding of the universe and admitted that we may not be able to know everything. Unlike Hume, who dismissed all philosophical speculation about what was unknowable, Kant admitted that questions about unknowable things are useful and interesting and that matter may not be all there is, thereby allowing for religious faith and establishing a tradition of transcendentalism that would continue in the thought of Schelling, Coleridge, Emerson, and others. Broadly speaking, Kant set the stage for the more idealist aspects of nineteenth-century Romanticism in Europe and America.

Wordsworth and Coleridge could not find in empiricism a satisfactory way of thinking about creativity: Coleridge once wrote that 'the Souls of 500 Sir Isaac Newtons would go to the making up of a Shakspeare or a Milton' (*Letters* 2: 709). Wordsworth wanted to combine Locke's emphasis on the primacy of sensory experience with a more mystical and subjective way of thinking about the natural world. As a creative artist, he was interested, like Coleridge, in the power of the imagination and the workings of the mind, particularly memory; unlike Coleridge, he felt no powerful connection to religion until later in life that could account for the 'sense sublime' he felt in communion with nature. Both writers were interested in understanding how the mind arrives at moral knowledge and virtue. For a time the two poets shared enthusiasm for David Hartley's *Observations on Man, His Frame, His Duty, and His Expectations* (1749), which developed Locke's empiricism into associationism. Hartley was interested in the way the mind arrives at knowledge by receiving sensation and then associating those sensations with ideas, explaining that the physical experience of pain and pleasure can lead to complex concepts such as sympathy, morality, and even God. The influence of Hartley is evident in Wordsworth's poem 'Expostulation and Reply' when he writes that 'we can feed this mind of ours, / In a wise passiveness,' that the physical experience of nature can provide moral sustenance without actively seeking instruction. He also explains in the Preface to *Lyrical Ballads* that one of the volume's 'principal objects' was to illustrate 'the manner in which we associate ideas in a state of excitement' (*LBRW* 392). But Hartley's associationism was limited to passive reception, and both Wordsworth and Coleridge believed that the imagination had a creative influence on the way we perceive the world and on how we remember our experiences. As we look more closely at specific Wordsworth poems, we will see the Enlightenment influence emerge again and again as he celebrates 'the mighty world / Of eye and ear, both what they half-create, / And what perceive' ('Tintern Abbey' 106–8). Locke and Hartley lay behind the emphasis on the senses, but the subjective, imaginative power to 'half-create' is the Romantic innovation of Wordsworth and Coleridge.

Wordsworth would write about feelings and memories and about sublime, transcendent experiences throughout his entire career, frequently coming tantalizingly close to what seems like a poetic philosophy of the way the mind combines perception, memory, and imagination. Philosophers might accuse Wordsworth of being a bad philosopher, a vocation for which he never claimed a calling. He was certainly a thinker, although perhaps not a systematic one. In some ways a Platonic essentialist, and ultimately a more conventional Anglican Christian, Wordsworth could not accept that 'there are no fixed principles in human nature' and would have harsh words for the Scottish empiricists Smith and Hume (*MW* 649). But he was never committed to the love of knowledge so much as he was to fidelity to 'the feelings of human nature,' as he wrote in a letter to a young admirer, feelings that defy reasonable explanation: according to Wordsworth,

a great Poet . . . ought to a certain degree to rectify men's feel-
ings, to give them new compositions of feeling, to render their
feelings more sane pure and permanent, in short, more con-
sonant to nature, that is, to eternal nature, and the great
moving spirit of things. (*MW* 622)

In his poetry, he never pretends to know more than he does, and
for those who admire his poetry this may be his saving grace. In
'Expostulation and Reply' and 'The Tables Turned,' companion
poems written, as he tells us in the 1798 'Advertisement' to
Lyrical Ballads, for a friend (William Hazlitt) who was 'some-
what unreasonably attached to modern books of moral philoso-
phy,' Wordsworth criticizes analytical thinking in favor of a 'wise
passiveness,' believing that the mindless pleasure one takes in
nature leads inevitably to virtue:

> One impulse from a vernal wood
> May teach you more of man;
> Of moral evil and of good,
> Than all the sages can.
>
> Sweet is the lore which nature brings;
> Our meddling intellect
> Misshapes the forms of beauteous things;
> —We murder to dissect.
>
> Enough of science and of art;
> Close up those barren leaves;
> Come forth, and bring with you a heart
> That watches and receives. ('The Tables Turned' 21–32)

These three stanzas capture many of the threads in this chapter:
Wordsworth exchanges Godwinian moral philosophy for 'one
impulse from a vernal wood'; he critiques the scientific method
of inquiry, 'the meddling intellect,' that established the Enlight-
enment; he echoes Rousseau's doubt that the arts and sciences
have improved society; and, finally, he employs ideas on percep-
tion influenced by Locke and Hartley to express his own vision
of how communion with nature, what he later calls 'a Spirit in
the woods' ('Nutting' 54), may renovate humanity. Wordsworth's

verse catches him at moments both of certainty and doubt, although he may seem certain more often than not. But the doubt is present from an early poem such as 'Lines Written in Early Spring' (1798), in which he acknowledges that this communion frequently does lead to a sad wisdom about humankind, 'what man has made of man.' Or ten years later, in 'Elegiac Stanzas,' where he must confront the possibility that nature sometimes does betray the heart that loves her. If one considers *The Prelude* as Wordsworth's ultimate statement on nature and humanity, the certainty resounds the loudest; here, it is not dogmatic—though it frequently finds its expression in the religious-sounding language of faith. More accurately, it is the language of perception at a particular moment, an early form of impressionism perhaps—like Constable's cloud studies. It is only the recurrence of certain interrogations that make his articulations seem like articles of faith. But on a fundamental level, Wordsworth's poetry is about making a connection between the poet and the reader, and then hopefully with a larger spirit of humanity: it asks of its reader only 'a heart / That watches and receives.' Although he is thought of as a Nature poet—sometimes, indeed, Nature-worshipper—Wordsworth's poetry is concerned primarily with exploring the belief that, as he writes in 'The Old Cumberland Beggar,' 'we have all of us one human heart' (146).

FOR FURTHER STUDY

1. Prior to the publication of *Lyrical Ballads*, Coleridge was more publicly engaged in political writing than Wordsworth was; as they both turned away from the French Revolution, their writing became more humanitarian and less specifically political. But *Lyrical Ballads* does contain hints throughout of their previous radical engagements: how do the poems 'The Female Vagrant' and 'The Convict' reveal a more overt political agenda than do the other poems in *Lyrical Ballads*?

2. One of Wordsworth's earlier poems to be included in *Lyrical Ballads*, 'Lines Left upon a Seat in a Yew-Tree' was composed in 1797 after Wordsworth had renounced Godwin's cold intellectualism. Putting aside whatever notions you have of Romanticism, how might you read this as a poem of the Enlightenment? A phrase such as 'one soft impulse' seems to

recall Locke and Hartley (see also 'Expostulation and Reply' and 'The Tables Turned,' also from *Lyrical Ballads*) and the term 'faculties' (49) seems to imply mental ones. Given the debate between empiricists and rationalists regarding knowledge, what does Wordsworth mean when he instructs the traveler/reader to 'be wiser thou! Instructed that true knowledge leads to love'? Which knowledge is true and which is false?

CHAPTER 2

STYLE, LANGUAGE, AND FORM

In one of the notes to the 1800 *Lyrical Ballads*, Wordsworth writes that 'the Reader cannot be too often reminded that Poetry is passion' (*LBRW* 389). For Wordsworth, passion in poetry is not merely the subject of a poem but also the means of its expression and its resultant effect. He believes strongly that the language, style, and form of a poem essentially achieve the passion the poem means to convey. For many readers, however, the actual qualities of Wordsworth's style may be elusive. Wordsworth gave much thought to how he wanted his poetry to work on readers, not only to what he wanted to say to them, while at the same time doggedly pursuing his aesthetic of simplicity and a stripping away of ornamentation so that the style becomes invisible. Commenting on Wordsworth in 1879, Matthew Arnold wrote, 'It might seem that Nature not only gave him the matter for his poem, but wrote the poem for him. He has no style' ('Mr Wordsworth' 155). Indeed, Wordsworth believed that the language of poetry should be no different than prose, while maintaining a commitment to other formal and generic expectations for poetic practice. In other words, Wordsworth still wants to write poetry that people will read as poetry, but he wants to alter the terms of the generic contract, what he calls the 'formal engagement' a poet makes with his reader by choosing to write poetry. This chapter sets up the basic tenets of Wordsworth's views on poetry; the next chapter will examine in depth his practice.

Wordsworth largely is responsible for changing the idiom of poetry from deliberate artificiality to something more like the way people actually speak. But during the 1790s Wordsworth's admitted experiments with more conversational language raised suspicions in some readers about the political and social implications of his poetry. While it is possible to enjoy his poetry without much regard to politics, readers always should remember that there is something fundamentally political in Wordsworth's

1798 'Advertisement' to *Lyrical Ballads*, where he explains that his purpose is to adapt 'the language of conversation of the middle and lower classes . . . for the purposes of poetic pleasure.' Years later, critic William Hazlitt said that Wordsworth's 'Muse . . . is a levelling one. It proceeds on a principle of equality, and strives to reduce all things to the same standard' ('Mr Wordsworth' 161). As far as his 'levelling Muse' is concerned in practice, even at the level of language, Wordsworth's poetry asserts an egalitarian claim. Wordsworth is most famous for his criticism of ornate, overly elaborate poetic diction and his practice of using simpler, humbler language; the 'levelling' a reader sees in poetic technique points to a more overtly political engagement as he develops his literary agenda during the 1790s. But Wordsworth ultimately asserted that what his critics perceived as a class issue was more a matter of aesthetic truth. The formal engagement supersedes the political one.

Many of Wordsworth's contemporary critics also saw his style as a degradation of literature. In 1807, Wordsworth's great antagonist, the critic Francis Jeffrey, for example, complained that 'new poets' such as Wordsworth were 'furnishing themselves from vulgar ballads and plebeian nurseries' when they ought to be 'borrowing from the more popular passages of their illustrious predecessors' (Woof 189). What Jeffrey really seems worked up about is the potential 'levelling' of poetic decorum in the borrowing from illegitimate sources. After 17 years of critical abuse, what he calls 'unremitting hostility,' Wordsworth defends his practice in the Preface to his 1815 collection of *Poems* and points out that 'every Author, as far as he is great and at the same time *original*, has had the task of *creating* the taste by which he is to be enjoyed' (*MW* 657–8). Although he was writing out of frustration with the taste of his time and his sense of being unpopular, Wordsworth's eventual success made it impossible for poets to return to the artificial diction of the past and have any hope of capturing the interest of readers. Creating taste finally is more a matter of style than substance, particularly Wordsworth's poetry of the so-called great decade, 1798–1807. In later chapters, we shall see the implications of Wordsworth's stylistic and generic agenda for his work of 'the great decade,' especially *Lyrical Ballads*, and for his sense of his vocation and legacy as a poet.

POETIC DICTION

In terms of style, Wordsworth's most important legacy is his rejection of eighteenth-century poetic diction. He lamented 'the artifices which have overrun our writings in metre since the days of Dryden and Pope' (*Prose* 2: 84). While he was not the first to write in a simpler, more conversational style, he was the first to be mercilessly attacked for doing so as a fundamental principle (see Chapter 4). His most famous articulation of this principle is the Preface to *Lyrical Ballads*, which first appeared in the second edition of 1800 and which Wordsworth expanded in 1802; it is customary to read the Preface to *Lyrical Ballads* as something of a manifesto for Wordsworth's poetry (and for Romanticism as well). Readers should keep in mind, however, that the Preface is not really a blueprint for *Lyrical Ballads*. Wordsworth wrote it for the second edition in order to explain and defend the poetic principles he felt he shared with Coleridge in writing the poems of the first edition. But for that first edition of 1798, Wordsworth was already keen to announce the innovation he and Coleridge had developed, anticipating the shock his readers might feel in having the generic expectations surrounding their appreciation of the poetry thwarted. The 1798 *Lyrical Ballads* opens with a 600-word 'Advertisement' that Wordsworth wrote to explain what the volume was attempting to accomplish:

> The majority of the following poems are to be considered as experiments. They were written chiefly with a view to ascertain how far the language of conversation in the middle and lower classes of society is adapted to the purposes of poetic pleasure. Readers accustomed to the gaudiness and inane phraseology of many modern writers, if they persist in reading this book to its conclusion, will perhaps frequently have to struggle with feelings of strangeness and aukwardness [*sic*]: they will look round for poetry, and will be induced to enquire by what species of courtesy these attempts can be permitted to assume that title. (*LBRW* 21)

What is experimental here is not so much the use of 'the language of conversation in the middle and lower classes of society' in poetry; so-called peasant poets Stephen Duck, Ann Yearsley, and, of course, Robert Burns had already introduced working-class vernacular into poetry; and the ballad revival that began with Thomas Percy's popular 1765 collection *Reliques of Ancient English Poetry* had already familiarized folk traditions to an educated, literary readership. The novelty is the conscious, deliberate 'adaptation' of it by two poets well-versed in the conventions of what we would call today 'high culture.' Wordsworth understands that he is radically challenging the expectations his readers have for poetry, but he wants them to give the 'experiment' the benefit of the doubt in the hope that they will find in *Lyrical Ballads* 'poetic pleasure' and 'a natural delineation of human passions, human characters, and human incidents' (21). Wordsworth here is following Rousseau, who believed that language began as poetry, in the passionate utterance of primitive people who felt before they thought. No less a poetic genius than Burns himself had capitalized on the novelty of his poetic persona, 'the heaven-taught ploughman,' as a kind of poetic noble savage, which many readers considered merely a charming literary curiosity. But Wordsworth is making a more significant play not only in promoting a simpler style of language but also in challenging 'our own pre-established codes of decision'—the prevailing standards of taste. And this includes an attack on what he deems 'the gaudiness and inane phraseology of many modern writers.'

Wordsworth, as it turns out, has first-hand experience with 'gaudiness and inane phraseology,' having employed some himself in his early poetry. He does not specify which 'modern writers' he finds guilty of the charge, although we might look directly at the popular poetry associated with Robert Merry, who wrote under the pen-name 'Della Crusca,' from the 1780s and into the 1790s. The highly ornate style of the Della Cruscans, as they were called, had been ferociously attacked by satirist William Gifford in his 1791 poem *The Baviad* as 'false glare, incongruous images . . . noise, and nonsense' (39–40). Reviewers of *Lyrical Ballads* immediately perceived a departure from the Della Cruscans as well: one magazine, the *Monthly Mirror*, praised Wordsworth's and Coleridge's volume for its 'sentiments of feeling and sensibility, expressed without affectation' in contrast to the 'pompous and high-sounding phraseology of the *Della Cruscan school*' (*LBRW* 351). Yet, Wordsworth's own first major publication, *An Evening Walk*, published in 1793 but begun four years earlier, shows a young poet trying to establish himself by showing his mastery of the prevailing style for poetry—the Della Cruscan. Read in its own context, it is an impressive first book, full of allusions to and echoes of such poets as Milton, Spenser, Thomson, Cowper, and Charlotte Smith. But read in relation to Wordsworth's later strictures on poetry, particularly the Preface to *Lyrical Ballads*, it reveals many stylistic tendencies—particularly inverted syntax and allegorical personifications of abstract ideas such as Content, Quiet, Hope, and Memory—that readers since the Preface find difficult to appreciate. For example, Wordsworth's passage describing a rooster on a mountain farm is hilariously bad, overwrought as it seems to us today:

> Sweetly ferocious round his native walks,
> Gazed by his sister-wives, the monarch stalks;
> Spur-clad his nervous feet, and firm his tread,
> A crest of purple tops his warrior head.
> Bright sparks his black and haggard eye-ball hurls
> Afar his tail he closes and unfurls;
> Whose state, like pine-trees, waving to and fro,
> Droops, and o'er canopies his regal brow,
> On tiptoe reared he blows his clarion throat,
> Threatened by faintly answering farms remote. (129–38)

In the eighteenth century, readers were likely to be pleased by the elaborate and surprising inventiveness of the description. To us today, the effect is gimmicky and pretentious, but it is important to remember that Wordsworth published the poem hoping to make money from it because he knew he had written it in a style that suited the tastes of contemporary poetry consumers.

It would take a few years for Wordsworth to realize that the conventional poetic language he himself had used—phrases such as 'finny flood' (for fishing stream) or 'fleecy store' (for sheep)—was no longer sufficient ('Salisbury Plain' 228, 233). He would come to the conclusion that ornamental language interferes with the poem's ability to communicate truth. By 1795, Coleridge had begun adopting a more conversational style influenced by William Cowper's *The Task* for his poetry, thus influencing Wordsworth in turn. Coleridge's influence on Wordsworth's diction is apparent in such 'conversation poems' by Coleridge as

'The Eolian Harp,' 'Fears in Solitude,' 'Frost at Midnight' and 'The Nightingale,' the last of which appeared in *Lyrical Ballads*. And in the Preface to *Lyrical Ballads*, Wordsworth singles out for attack a sonnet by Thomas Gray that contains many similar poeticisms to those above, going so far as to select only five of the 14 lines as having 'any value' because they are free of the 'curiously elaborate' poetic diction found in the rest of the text (*LBRW* 397–8). Wordsworth defends his rejection of poetic language on the grounds that 'the language of a large portion of every good poem, even of the most elevated character, must necessarily, except with reference to the metre, in no respect differ from that of good prose' (*LBRW* 397). A reviewer of the second edition of *Lyrical Ballads* described Wordsworth's earlier poetry as 'obscured by diction, often and intentionally inflated,' but recognized the value of the innovation announced in *Lyrical Ballads*: 'His style is now wholly changed, and he has adopted a purity of expression, which, to the fastidious ear, may sometimes sound poor and low, but which is infinitely more correspondent with true feeling than what, by the courtesy of the day, is usually called poetical language' (Woof 138). For at least one critic, Wordsworth made an important change in poetic expression; but for others, the rejection of 'poetical language' was a major defect of this and several of Wordsworth's subsequent volumes.

But giving Wordsworth all the credit for banishing gimmicky poetic diction risks burying the influence of eighteenth-century poets such as Mark Akenside, Joseph Warton, and William Collins—and more immediately that of Charlotte Smith, Coleridge, and William Cowper. As we pursue Wordsworth's late-eighteenth-century influences, surprising connections will continue to come to light. During the 1990s scholars such as William D. Brewer and Mary F. Yudin, for example, re-examined playwright Joanna Baillie's 'Introductory Discourse' to her 1798 volume, *A Series of Plays*, showing how it shares many of the same concerns with poetic language, and how it prefigures Wordsworth's expanded prefaces to *Lyrical Ballads* in 1800 and 1802. In response to the ever-increasing readership of novels, Baillie, too, advocates the representation of 'human nature in the middling and lower classes of society' and warns that figurative language and poetic diction—what she calls 'all this decoration and ornament, all this loftiness and refinement'—will make poetry irrelevant to more and more readers who expect from literature the pleasure 'derived from the sympathetick interest we all take in beings like ourselves' (*LBRW* 165–6). Wordsworth similarly asserts, 'Poets do not write for Poets alone, but for men'; the poet, therefore, 'must express himself as other men express themselves' (*LBRW* 404). For the prefaces to *Lyrical Ballads*, Wordsworth may have 'silently borrowed' from Baillie, as Paula R. Feldman suggests (22). Moreover, these ideas may have been the inevitable result of the rise of the novel and revolutionary politics coinciding in the second half of the eighteenth century.

'FORMAL ENGAGEMENT'

In the Preface to *Lyrical Ballads*, Wordsworth shifts the discussion of diction from class in the original 1798 'Advertisement'— 'the language of conversation in the middle and lower classes of society'—via the more general 'selection of language really used by men,' to a more specific emphasis on genre (*LBRW* 392). Obviously, he is invested in the act of writing poetry, not prose. Wordsworth is a much more formal poet than he may appear to be at first; by calling him formal, I mean to emphasize that his selection of poetic form—simple lyric, sonnet, ode, blank-verse meditation, epic—is far from arbitrary and that his techniques— meter, rhyme, syntax, enjambment—deliberately serve and enhance the meaning of his poems. He admits that 'by the act of writing in verse,' the poet 'makes a formal engagement': an implicit agreement that the poet will 'gratify' the reader's expectations for what poetry usually says and does. To some readers of *Lyrical Ballads*, it may seem that he has not 'fulfilled the terms of an engagement thus voluntarily contracted' (*LBRW* 391–2). He establishes that poetic diction should not differ from the language of prose, so he must go on to justify the arrangement of words in meter, stanza, and rhyme. If he employs, as he repeatedly asserts, 'the language really spoken by men,' Wordsworth must then explain how this accords with the use of other artifices of verse composition that are foreign to conversation or prose.

Wordsworth is a poet of pleasure. Wordsworth's poetry springs from his own pleasure, and it has no more important object than the giving of pleasure to his readers. But as we have seen, he is aware that his style likely will challenge his readers' expectations and thus may interfere with their receiving pleasure from the poetry. If his diction is no different from that of prose or of ordinary conversation, Wordsworth calls upon his imagination and his poetic skills to make the poems interesting and pleasurable. In the Preface to *Lyrical Ballads*, Wordsworth writes that his 'principal object' was 'to chuse incidents and situations from common life' and 'to throw over them a certain colouring of imagination, whereby ordinary things should be presented to the mind in an unusual way' (*LBRW* 392). But because he hopes 'to keep my Reader in the company of flesh and blood, persuaded that by so doing I shall interest him,' he abandons poetic conventions such as 'personifications of abstract ideas' (except in the occasional case of 'a figure of speech . . . prompted by passion') and 'falsehood of description' (perhaps like his rooster above) (396). Style and substance, he suggests, are frequently at odds in the poetry of other writers; so, how can he reconcile them?

Wordsworth still wants to preserve the elements of poetry that he believes enhance passion and pleasure. Tools of poetry such as meter and rhyme obviously contribute to any poem's effect; but Wordsworth understands, as he explains in a letter to John Thelwall, that 'the passion of metre'—that is, the way the words are organized into metrical units—may create sonic effects 'not called out for by the passion of the subject' (*Early Years* 434). The problem is how to make 'the passion of metre' and 'the passion of the subject' work in tandem. Managing the effect of meter and rhyme is a subtle skill that justifies the poetic practice laid out in the Preface to *Lyrical Ballads*. One of the most abstruse sections of the Preface shows the difficulty Wordsworth has in explaining how, in Pope's words, 'the sound must seem an echo to the sense' (*Essay on Criticism* 365). For Wordsworth, sound (meter) and sense (meaning) have a complex psychological interrelationship because of the excitement, the emotions, the pain or pleasure, poetry imparts to the reader. Wordsworth wants his poetry to be an emotional experience for the reader, but he wants to distinguish it from the overly effusive, soggy manner of the Della Cruscans, whose style he would consider to be not 'manly.' He is concerned that, without some restraint, 'the excitement may be carried beyond its proper bounds.' The restraint is provided by form, which acts along with the excitement produced by 'the passion of the subject': 'the co-presence of something regular,' such as meter and rhyme, he writes, will have 'great efficacy in tempering and restraining the passion' (*LBRW* 405–6). This is what makes poetry art: while he wants to strip away ornamental language in order to facilitate apprehension, Wordsworth is not after realism; he does not want the chaos of emotion, sensibility, to interfere with the pleasure of receiving artistic expression, so he admits that the formal construction of sentiment as poetry will 'divest language in a certain degree of its reality' and 'will throw a sort of half consciousness of unsubstantial existence over the whole composition' (406). Although he does not say so explicitly, the effect he describes is dream-like in the suggestion that versification aids the achievement of a subconscious pleasure. In addition to the ways in which ideas expressed in rhyme may give the impression of being more deeply true, Wordsworth suggests that the regularity of meter orders the emotional matter so that it may give more pleasure—particularly if, as is the case with many of the *Lyrical Ballads* (such as 'The Last of the Flock,' 'The Mad Mother,' or 'Ruth'), the pathos associated with the subjects may be painfully unpleasant. Rhyme and meter, or 'the music of harmonious metrical language,' temper 'the painful feeling which will always be found intermingled with powerful descriptions of the deeper passions' (407). Conversely, in poems on lighter subjects, according to Wordsworth, the 'ease and gracefulness with which the Poet manages his numbers' (or meter) is the 'principal source of the gratification of the Reader' (407). So, in other words, versification makes painful subjects more endurable and lighter subjects more artful. This is why, where the subject is the same, 'the verse will be read a hundred times where the prose is read once' (408). The formal characteristics of poetry, then, give ideas greater longevity than if they were expressed in prose.

'SPONTANEOUS OVERFLOW OF POWERFUL FEELING'

This point leads to a common misconception about Wordsworth, his Preface, and the Romantics in general—that Romantic poetry is the unthinking, unrestrained *gurges* of emotion. Such a caricature is largely due to one of Wordsworth's most memorable phrases, 'the spontaneous overflow of powerful feelings,' which he uses twice in the Preface. Most readers remember his claim that 'all good poetry is the spontaneous overflow of powerful feeling' but forget his subsequent qualifications. Without those qualifications, Wordsworth's phrase would seem to legitimize a lot of really terrible adolescent poetry. But as his attention to form confirms, Wordsworth did not believe poetry only to be an outpouring of emotion, nor did he think of *spontaneous* as unpremeditated or impulsive. He is describing, instead, the act of composition, in which a poet voluntarily summons powerful feeling in order to furnish the poem with 'a worthy *purpose*' (393). Overflow, moreover, is not the same as overspill: the 'powerful feeling' originates as 'emotion recollected in tranquillity' [*sic*] (407). The operations of the mind ('our thoughts') reconstitute the emotion so that the poet finds himself in 'a state of enjoyment' conducive to composition and through contemplation discovers 'what is really important to men' (407, 394). Wordsworth offers a poetic description of this process in the opening book of *The Prelude*, where he describes pouring out his 'soul in measured strains'; he writes, 'poetic numbers came / Spontaneously' (1.57, 60–1). Note the emphasis on metrical restraint, on how his powerful feeling comes under the ordinance of his craft.

The evolution from the 1798 Advertisement to the 1802 Preface parallels the movement from what M. H. Abrams calls the eighteenth-century 'pragmatic' theory, which considers poetry's effect on the audience to be the goal, to what has come to be thought of as the more Romantic or 'expressive' theory of art, which Abrams describes as 'the internal made external' (*Mirror* 22). The Preface also exhibits Wordsworth's emerging conception of himself as a poet. As the passages added in 1802 show, Wordsworth thought of the poet, and of himself, as 'a man speaking to men' but also as a man who possesses 'more lively sensibility, more enthusiasm and tenderness, who has a greater knowledge of human nature, and a more comprehensive soul, than are supposed to be common among mankind' (399). But again Wordsworth wants to distinguish himself from the poet of Sensibility whose emotions, or 'immediate external excitement,' occasion an unthinking poem; and while he believes that the poet is inherently gifted to a certain extent, he also asserts that the poet has to earn his position through practice and skill, acquiring thus 'a greater readiness and power in expressing what he thinks and feels' (400).

WORDSWORTH'S FORMS: LYRIC AND BALLAD

Wordsworth's careful attention to form belies the misconception of his poetry as merely 'the spontaneous overflow of powerful feeling.' Wordsworth, like many of the great poets who preceded him—Virgil, Ovid, Dante, Petrarch, Milton—had a keen understanding of the relationship between poetic form and poetic fame. The poetry of 'the great decade' illustrates the competing claims upon him as he shaped a poetic identity, the tension between his enjoyment of writing in shorter lyric forms and his ambition to write longer, narrative works. Even the title *Lyrical Ballads* implies a principle that I elsewhere have called 'formal paradoxy' in the juxtaposition of two contrasting, even contradictory forms, the lyric and the ballad. The lyric is classical in origin, deriving from Greek songs sung to the accompaniment of a lyre; these are short poems that develop subjective themes, insights, emotions. The ballad has folk origins and is narrative; it tells a story in a rustic vernacular. Both forms take their origin in music and therefore rhyme (as songs today do). The ballad had become popular again with the publication in 1765 of Percy's hugely successful *Reliques of Ancient English Poetry*. By the time *Lyrical Ballads* appeared the ballad was ubiquitous, so much so that Wordsworth, in the Preface, suggests that what 'distinguishes these Poems from the popular Poetry of the day' is that they are ballads that are uniquely *lyrical* in the emphasis on the subjective experience of the speakers, who may or may not be adequate narrators: he explains that in *Lyrical Ballads* 'the feeling therein developed gives importance to the action and situation, and not the action and situation to the feeling' (*LBRW* 394–5). Plot is subordinate to lyrical insight, in other words. But also, as Paul Sheats suggests, plot is subordinate to the lyrical versatility of Wordsworth's variously impassioned meters (185). Sheats, moreover, is correct in reminding us that, in the case of the 1798 *Lyrical Ballads*, which employ throughout narrators who are not necessarily the poet, Wordsworth's practice, using Abrams' terms, is still pragmatic and not yet expressive (280). But these distinctions are what make the tension between *lyric* and *ballad* so compelling in Wordsworth's first major collection, particularly in a poem such as 'Simon Lee' or 'The Thorn' (see Chapter 3).

After the 1798 *Lyrical Ballads* Wordsworth's poetry shows a greater distinction between lyric and narrative modes. The 1800 *Lyrical Ballads* and the 1807 *Poems, in Two Volumes* also contain some of Wordsworth's finest lyrics, though their excellences reveal themselves in more subtle ways than in paradoxical formal juxtapositions. These poems are more identifiable as traditional lyrics that develop the particular insight or emotion of a single speaker. But, as with all of Wordsworth's poetry, even the simplest-seeming poem may yield interpretable ambiguities. The 'Lucy' poems from 1800, for example, are mini symbolist masterpieces in their sparse but suggestive language, intense imagery, and psychological depth (these include the poems beginning 'Strange fits of passion,' 'She dwelt among th' untrodden ways,' 'A slumber did my spirit seal'). Wordsworth's interest in the lyric by 1807 led him to the ode, which is, at its most basic level, an extended, more formal and serious lyric poem; it was a robust form during the eighteenth century. For the 1807 volumes, Wordsworth produced two significant odes, his 'Intimations Ode,' widely regarded as his greatest poem, and the less familiar 'Ode to Duty,' which interestingly seems to contradict much of what Wordsworth says about his poetic principles in the Preface. I will discuss in greater depth a selection of the 1800 and 1807 lyrics in Chapter 3.

WORDSWORTH'S FORMS: EPIC AND SONNET

Wordsworth well knew that he would have to engage more traditionally difficult forms in order to follow in the footsteps of his great predecessors and, as his writing clearly shows, the one who haunted his imagination and ambition was Milton. Writing from his personal experience of his contemporary, Hazlitt wrote of Wordsworth that 'Milton is his great idol, and he sometimes dares to compare himself with him' ('Mr Wordsworth' 166). As a young man, Wordsworth wrote that, should he be able to write 'a narrative Poem of the Epic kind, I shall consider the *task* of my life as over' (*Early Years* 594–5). From the early days of their collaboration in 1798, Coleridge urged Wordsworth to write a great philosophical poem that would rival Milton's accomplishment in *Paradise Lost*. Their friend Southey had already completed the first draft of his epic poem *Madoc* by 1799 (published 1805). Wordsworth, however, showed no interest in the traditional trappings of epic heroism. After *Paradise Lost*, the massive scope of Milton's epic seemed impossible to match. Both Wordsworth and Coleridge felt the pressure to write a Miltonic epic, but Coleridge soon realized that Wordsworth was better equipped for the task. Influenced by Coleridge's wide-ranging intellect, Wordsworth conceived of *The Recluse* as a vehicle for conveying 'most of the knowledge of which I am possessed' in 'pictures of Nature, Man, and Society'; he writes in a letter, 'Indeed I know not any thing which will not come within the scope of my plan' (*Early Years* 212). It was to have been his great moral and philosophical poem. He never completed *The Recluse*, but he did write parts of it: only *The Excursion* (1814) appeared in print during Wordsworth's life; he wrote *Home at Grasmere* between 1800 and 1806, while working on *The Prelude*, and 'The Tuft of Primroses' in 1808. These poems appeared posthumously in 1888 and 1949 respectively. Kenneth R. Johnston's *Wordsworth and* The Recluse (1984) is a brilliant study of how all of these poems interrelate to give a sense of what the final project might have looked like.

Although he never completed what he believed was his proper epic project, Wordsworth's great innovation in the epic tradition is the turn inward—the subjective or expressive epic with the poet himself as hero-thinker. This he accomplishes in *The Prelude*, which is a kind of poetic autobiography that gives insight into Wordsworth's own view of himself and the development of his mind and his calling as a poet. It is the longest and most ambitious poem that Wordsworth completed. Begun out of frustration with his own lack of progress on *The Recluse*, *The Prelude*, which was not published until after Wordsworth's death (like Virgil's *Aeneid*), turns out to be the most significant contribution to the epic tradition after Milton and before James Joyce's *Ulysses*. The poem is an articulation of the love of knowledge—or, more specifically, of *knowing*—but it is a subjective one. It conveys the imaginative, psychological, aesthetic, and moral episteme that is at the heart of Wordsworth's poetry. It occupied his mind for half a century, from its inception in 1798 until his final revisions in the 1840s, and was finally published, according to his wishes, just weeks after his death in

1850. Wordsworth wrote *The Prelude* in tribute to Coleridge's confidence that Wordsworth would be one of the great poets and always referred to it as 'the poem to Coleridge'; but he also began it in the spirit of procrastination, deferring *The Recluse*, which he and Coleridge had started to plan while at Alfoxden. For many years Wordsworth resisted publishing *The Prelude* until he could actually begin and complete *The Recluse*, in a continuous cycle of poetic procrastination. When he published *The Excursion*, which was to be part of *The Recluse*, in 1814, Wordsworth explained in the Preface that he had completed an autobiographical poem that would have a relation to *The Recluse* 'as the Anti-chapel [*sic*] has to the body of a gothic church' (ix). This is one reason his wife, Mary, gave the poem its title for posthumous publication—*The Prelude; or Growth of a Poet's Mind*—as it serves as a kind of prelude to *The Recluse*. But it is also, as he explains in 1814, a 'preparatory Poem' that 'conducts the history of the Author's mind to the point when he was emboldened to hope that his faculties were sufficiently matured' for such an ambitious project. It is thanks to Coleridge, therefore, that he felt so 'emboldened.' But as the years wore on and *The Recluse* failed to materialize, Wordsworth decided that he did not wish *The Prelude* to appear in print until after his death because he was uncomfortable with 'the personal character of the subject' (*Later Years* 3: 680). Indeed, while working on an early version of his epic of the artist, he wrote to a friend that it is 'a thing unprecedented in Literary history that a man should talk so much about himself' (*Early Years* 586). Today, many readers enjoy reading autobiography, as the popularity of memoir as a genre in recent years demonstrates; *The Prelude*, while not exactly *Angela's Ashes*, may be ripe for today's appetites for the personal.

Wordsworth's collaboration with Coleridge and his increasingly epic ambitions coincide with another important stylistic or formal feature of Wordsworth's poetry. Wordsworth, after Shakespeare and Milton, is the most significant practitioner of blank verse, or unrhymed iambic pentameter. As Wordsworth created the taste by which he is to be enjoyed, Milton inaugurated blank verse as the standard for the English epic in contempt of 'the troublesome and modern bondage of rhyming' (291).

Blank verse proved during the eighteenth century to be particularly versatile in such long proto-Romantic poems as James Thomson's *The Seasons* (1726), Akenside's *The Pleasures of the Imagination* (1744), and Cowper's *The Task* (1785), the latter of which has a mock-epic quality and demonstrates Cowper's skill at managing blank verse with a mixture of colloquialism and formality, playfulness and seriousness. Following Cowper, Coleridge adapted blank verse for meditative poems, the 'conversation poems' mentioned above. Such uses of blank verse and conversational language would influence Wordsworth's 'Tintern Abbey' by showing how blank verse may convey lyrical insights much in the way an ode would do, but without intricate rhymes and stanzas. And, as he explained in a note to the poem in 1800, the poem has the general structure of an ode; and 'the impassioned music of [its] versification'—blank verse—substitutes for the formal qualities traditionally associated with an ode. Around the same time, Wordsworth began experimenting with the narrative potential of blank verse for such poems as 'The Ruined Cottage,' 'The Old Cumberland Beggar,' and his ironic pastorals, 'The Brothers' and 'Michael.' These narrative poems in blank verse are inextricably associated with the plan for *The Recluse* and with the composition of *The Prelude*.

This ambition metamorphoses into an anxiety that makes much of Wordsworth's writing of 'the great decade' seem indeed almost like procrastination even as he pushed technical and generic boundaries. Coleridge projected his epic ambitions onto Wordsworth, regularly checking on his progress and writing to him, 'of nothing but "The Recluse" can I hear patiently' (*Letters* 1: 538). *The Prelude* began as an apology of sorts from Wordsworth to Coleridge for his lack of progress, and Wordsworth worked intermittently on 'the poem to Coleridge' between 1799 and 1805, while also composing the lyrics for the 1800 *Lyrical Ballads* and the 1807 *Poems, in Two Volumes*. Coleridge meanwhile was chagrined, even hurt, that Wordsworth became interested in 'writing such a multitude of small Poems' instead of moving forward with *The Recluse* (*Letters* 2: 1013; see also *Letters* 1: 527). Coleridge's contempt for Wordsworth's lyric diversions recalls Samuel Johnson's comically pejorative definition of the sonnet as 'a small poem' and the sonneteer as 'a small poet' in his *Dictionary*.

Wordsworth never wrote *The Recluse*, but he did write more than 500 sonnets over the course of his career. Wordsworth perhaps transferred some of his epic anxieties onto a form about which he clearly felt more confident. Years later he recalled his sister's reading Milton's sonnets to him in 1802, reporting that he was struck with 'the dignified simplicity and majestic harmony' of them; Wordsworth 'took fire' and began, with his sonnet on Napoleon ('I grieved for Buonaparte'), his most extensive formal obsession (*Fenwick* 19). Like Milton (who only wrote 24 sonnets) Wordsworth almost exclusively writes in the Italian or Petrarchan form; this form is more difficult in English because it requires fewer rhymes than the English or Shakespearean sonnet, which was known in the eighteenth century as the 'illegitimate' sonnet. In an 1833 letter, Wordsworth explained his preference for Milton, who disrupts the rhetorical division of the Italian sonnet through the enjambment of the octave and the sestet and creates what Wordsworth refers to as the 'intense Unity' of 'the image of an orbicular body,—a sphere—or a dew drop' (*Later Years* 2: 653). The structural importance of the sonnet as a symbol for its content helpfully applies to most of Wordsworth's sonnets as well.

The sonnet would become for Wordsworth a formal synecdoche for his principles of versification—the idea of form as poetic discipline and as shaping receptacle for the 'spontaneous overflow of powerful feeling.' In the postscript to his 1820 sonnet sequence *The River Duddon*, Wordsworth discusses the 'restriction which the frame of the Sonnet' has imposed upon him, 'narrowing unavoidably the range of thought, and precluding, though not without its advantages, many graces to which a freer movement of verse would naturally have led' (*River Duddon* 38). But Wordsworth clearly enjoyed working within the sonnet's intricate strictness as much as he seems to have been overwhelmed by the scope of *The Recluse*. While *The Recluse* is metaphorically 'a gothic Church,' Wordsworth frequently uses the image of the narrow room to describe the sonnet form and to show how comfortable he is in it. One of the things that so appealed to him about Milton's sonnets was what he described as the 'energetic and varied flow of sound crowding into narrow room' with 'the combined effect of rhyme and blank verse' (*Early Years* 379). In the 'Prefatory Sonnet' ('Nuns fret not at their convent's narrow room') that opens a series of sonnets in the 1807 volume, Wordsworth asserts his freedom and thus his virtuosity within the formal demands of the sonnet:

> In sundry moods, 'twas pastime to be bound
> Within the Sonnet's scanty plot of ground;
> Pleas'd if some Souls (for such there needs must be)
> Who have felt the weight of too much liberty,
> Should find short solace there, as I have found. (10–14)

The 'weight of too much liberty' similarly drives Wordsworth's poetic impulse in the first book of *The Prelude*, his longest and most successful poem. Due to the influence of the Preface to *Lyrical Ballads* readers may not think of Wordsworth as a conventionally formal poet, yet the sonnet and the epic are in some ways the most artificial of all forms. But, at the end of 'the great decade,' with *Lyrical Ballads* behind him, *The Recluse* nowhere near completion, and *The Prelude* unpublished, it was precisely in this narrow room where Wordsworth meant to distinguish himself and how, if all else failed, he felt he might claim poetic immortality.

FOR FURTHER STUDY

1. How might Wordsworth's phrases applied to composition—'spontaneous overflow of powerful feeling' and 'emotion recollected in tranquillity'—provide assistance in reading Wordsworth's poetry? How do the formal qualities of the poems reflect the relationship between these two phrases?
2. Most editions of Wordsworth reprint the 1802 Preface to *Lyrical Ballads*, which is approximately 11,500 words, or excerpts from it; the 1800 Preface is approximately 6,700 words, while the original Advertisement is around 600 words. For further study, compare these three statements and look for the elements Wordsworth preserved, eliminated, or added.
3. How does 'Ode to Duty' (*MW* 295) stylistically contradict Wordsworth's stated principles in the Preface?
4. Compare Wordsworth's 1807 'Prefatory Sonnet,' beginning 'Nuns fret not at their convent's narrow room' (*MW* 286), with his 1827 sonnet beginning 'Scorn not the Sonnet' (*MW* 356); consider the ways in which both poems reflect what Harold

Bloom calls the 'anxiety of influence' or the ways in which they reveal a particularly confident Wordsworth making the case for his own greatness.

5. See Wordsworth's poem 'A Poet's Epitaph' (*MW* 151) for an uncharacteristically sarcastic and satirical poem; consider how it differs stylistically from what seem to be more typically Wordsworthian poems.

CHAPTER 3

READING WORDSWORTH'S POETRY

Wordsworth's career spans more than 50 years and includes hundreds of poems, so this chapter will focus on those works that general readers and students encounter most often. Wordsworth's most significant compositions and publications occurred during what scholars generally refer to as 'the great decade' of 1798 to 1807. As later editions of his *Poetical Works* show, Wordsworth himself preferred not to compartmentalize his poetry according to chronology or by original book publication, choosing instead to present his work thematically. For the purposes of understanding Wordsworth in the context of Romanticism, it may be more helpful, and likely more interesting, to concentrate on this period of intense creativity and deeply engaged interaction with Coleridge. My approach in this chapter is to focus on the three books of poetry Wordsworth published during this decade—the 1798 *Lyrical Ballads*, the expanded, two-volume 1800 *Lyrical Ballads*, and the 1807 *Poems, in Two Volumes*. During this decade Wordsworth figures out what it means to be Wordsworth, doing so publicly with the innovative poems of *Lyrical Ballads* and the famous preface that established his poetic principles, but also privately with the ongoing composition of his poetic autobiography *The Prelude*. In consideration of length, I have excluded from this chapter specific commentary on Wordsworth's epic masterpiece, *The Prelude*, which he completed in 1805 but did not publish until a greatly revised version appeared after his death in 1850. But I also believe it is important to focus on Wordsworth presenting himself to the public before one can study in depth the poet in private and in process. (The exception below is 'The Ruined Cottage,' which I will discuss in terms of the *Lyrical Ballads* collaboration.) While by the end of 'the great decade' he found himself to be something of a literary pariah, representing in the eyes of critics a deplorable new school of poetry, it is in fact largely the work of this period that has made him pre-eminent among the British Romantic poets. This chapter will begin with two demonstrations of how to read Wordsworth thematically, philosophically, and formally—two interpretive 'anchors': 'I Wandered Lonely as a Cloud,' or 'Daffodils,' and 'The Ruined Cottage.' From there, we will move on to the three books that make up this major part of the Wordsworth canon, focusing on some of their representative poems.

SECTION ONE: DEALING WITH THE DAFFODILS

The single greatest obstacle for reading and appreciating Wordsworth's poetry may be the daffodils. The poem commonly called by its first line 'I Wandered Lonely as a Cloud' or just 'Daffodils' (as Wordsworth himself referred to it) is immortalized on many a refrigerator magnet and persists as a staple of elementary school poetry recitals. From the poem's first publication, though, it was ridiculed as unworthy, even downright silly; to poet Anna Seward the poem produced 'astonishment and disgust' (Woof 250). Even Coleridge used it as an example of defect in Wordsworth's poetry (*Biographia* 2: 136). But 'I Wandered Lonely as a Cloud' remains one of Wordsworth's most famous poems, preserved in the pages of countless best-loved-poems-of-all-time anthologies. So there must be something to it to have such longevity and general appeal. But is it a good poem? Is it representative of Wordsworth's work?

It is on both counts. And it provides a starting point for reading Wordsworth's poetry and learning how to appreciate it. On our way to dealing with its questions and problems, we can identify useful approaches to Wordsworth in general. First of all, in discussing this poem, we have to make sure that we know which version of the poem we are reading. The most common version of the poem, the one in most anthologies, is the four-stanza poem Wordsworth presented in his first collected edition of 1815. But this is actually a revised and expanded version of the poem, which Wordsworth first published in 1807. The poem appeared without a title in the second volume of *Poems, in Two Volumes*; there, it is identified only as the seventh in a series of poems called 'Moods of My Own Mind.' In its original form, it has only three stanzas:

I wandered lonely as a Cloud
That floats on high o'er Vales and Hills,

When all at once I saw a crowd
A host of dancing Daffodils;
Along the Lake, beneath the trees,
Ten thousand dancing in the breeze.

The waves beside them danced, but they
Outdid the sparkling waves in glee:—
A Poet could not but be gay
In such a laughing company:
I gaz'd—and gaz'd—but little thought
What wealth the shew to me had brought:

For oft when on my couch I lie
In vacant or in pensive mood,
They flash upon that inward eye
Which is the bliss of solitude,
And then my heart with pleasure fills,
And dances with the Daffodils.

Poems, in Two Volumes is Wordsworth's first book of all-new poems since *Lyrical Ballads* in 1798; even though the subsequent editions of *Lyrical Ballads* had many more poems by Wordsworth than by Coleridge, we still think of the *Lyrical Ballads* project as a collaborative enterprise. How might the works in *Poems, in Two Volumes*, such as the one under consideration, reveal a different aesthetic than those in *Lyrical Ballads*, which contained many narrative poems? The later volume consists of many more lyric poems, including a good number of sonnets, and closes with Wordsworth's 'Intimations Ode,' which is considered by some to be his greatest poem. Certainly, the title Wordsworth gives to the poems in this particular series, 'Moods of My Own Mind,' would indicate an emphasis on the poet's subjective experience and on the traditional lyric representation of a speaker's mood, thoughts, perceptions, feelings, etc. So, unlike poems from *Lyrical Ballads* such as 'The Thorn' and 'We Are Seven' that have character-speakers, not the poet himself, these later poems announce themselves as emerging from Wordsworth's experience. And the daffodils poem explicitly draws attention to the speaker as poet in the ninth line. We are actually in more traditional lyric territory than we frequently find ourselves in

Lyrical Ballads, so we might want to consider how *Poems, in Two Volumes* reveals Wordsworth trying to do something different from what he had done before. Is the daffodils poem a break from what we see him doing in his earlier work? Or is it in line with where we see him going in poems on nature such as 'Lines Written at a Small Distance from my House,' 'Lines Written near Richmond, upon the Thames, at Evening,' or 'Nutting'? We might even find it difficult to understand how he could write such a sophisticated poem as 'Tintern Abbey' years earlier and then craft such a simple poem as this.

Readers, therefore, should consider Wordsworth's poetry in its original context first. Wordsworth was a professional writer who cared about the trajectory of his career and who wanted to be successful. But in 1807 he was also a creative artist who believed in his calling as a poet and would not compromise his aesthetic principles. While we cannot always speak confidently about authorial intention, it is safe to assume that the poet is trying to do something specific in his poem. So we need to read the poem for what it says about itself as a work of art. Since the original poem has no title, the emphasis is on the speaker first: he is wandering and he is lonely; in this way, he is like a cloud. The simile is actually surprising because clouds are not particularly solitary; the second line modifies the comparison and we understand that the separation is not from other clouds but from the earth itself. The figure thus emphasizes the speaker's disconnection from his own environment; the celestial imagery, moreover, implies a spiritual distance between the speaker and the physical world. But he is surprised by the sudden appearance of the daffodils, and just as suddenly the figurative language is interrupted as the reader becomes attached to the speaker's empirical observation and fairly literal description of the daffodils on the bank. The only remotely figurative expression in the stanza is the description of the flowers dancing. But this requires no great stretch of the imagination. Just as the speaker's eye is engaged in seeing the daffodils, we also understand that the very same agent that acts upon the flowers is the wind that would give the impression of a cloud wandering. The breeze has made a terrestrial connection 'along the lake, beneath the trees.' Subtly Wordsworth's diction, simple as it is, gives the impression of profound unity as every word seems to play off of every other word. In this way, readers may wish to view Wordsworth's poetry in light of Coleridge's ideas of organic form versus mechanic form, as well as his assertion that poetry is defined by its 'permitting a pleasure from the Whole consistent with a consciousness of pleasurable excitement from the component parts' (*Lectures* 1: 218). Similarly, in the Preface to the 1815 collection, Wordsworth writes at some length of the way his poetry attempts to bring 'into conjunction' the various powers of the imagination (*MW* 633). To consider a shared aesthetic between the two writers—even though they differ on specific points—is another useful way of reading Wordsworth's poetry.

This idea of unity and connection is a fundamental one in reading Wordsworth's poetry. And so is the application of the eye: you will notice that each stanza involves vision and visual imagery. The first two stanzas revolve around the action of the speaker seeing, as emphasized by the verbs 'saw' and 'gaz'd.' Like Locke and Hartley (see Chapter 1), Wordsworth is interested in what our minds do with what we see; but, like Blake, he is not interested in the limits of such knowledge because he understands that the imagination has great power to shape perception and memory. Obviously it is the speaker's perception of the scene that makes the flowers dance with the waves and outdo 'the sparkling waves in glee.' And note that the speaker 'little thought' at the time how important the experience of seeing the daffodils would be to him later. Wordsworth greatly values the emotional reception of stimulus—mood, feeling—and the power of the mind to replicate that experience in and of itself without the stimulus. For Wordsworth, this is what shapes a thinking and feeling human being, particularly a poet. And that is really what this poem is about—not the daffodils.

More specifically, the poem is about the poet's ability to turn ordinary experiences into something delightful or transcendent, not just for his use but for the reader's. According to Wordsworth, a poet is predisposed to feel deeply and then be able to process an experience intellectually in the act of composition. This is what has happened for Wordsworth, and his purpose is to show us the power of our own minds in the act of reading his poem. The third stanza takes us out of nature, brings us indoors with the poet 'in vacant or in pensive mood': here, it is the daffodils that activate the visual image—'They flash upon that inward eye.'

The mind's eye receives an image from the poet's memory—it is as if the daffodils themselves cause it to happen—and the poet is able to feel the same pleasure that he did when he saw them in person. The poem is simple; but for Wordsworth, the process described therein is sophisticated, and the power to *re*-view is essential in the most philosophical sense of the word.

Nature and Subjectivity

Wordsworth believes that we can learn, as he says in 'Tintern Abbey,' to 'see into the life of things.' The image of dancing daffodils, therefore, is more than figurative language and not just personification or 'pathetic fallacy'; it is a deeply held conviction that there is

>   a sense sublime
> Of something far more deeply interfused,
> Whose dwelling is the light of setting suns,
> And the round ocean, and the living air,
> And the blue sky, and in the mind of man,
> A motion and a spirit, that impels
> All thinking things, all objects of all thought,
> And rolls through all things. ('Tintern Abbey' 96–103)

Wordsworth wants to share with us his awareness of the underlying unity of all things. Obviously, in a long poem such as 'Tintern Abbey,' he can develop at length the intuitive element of this awareness, although he resists defining it more explicitly than 'something far more deeply interfused.' For Wordsworth the ability to perceive this 'motion' and 'spirit' is exercised first through the sensory experience of nature—as in seeing the daffodils by the lake—and then the activity 'in the mind of man.' This power 'impels' both animated, conscious nature and 'objects of all thought'—that is, anything that we can contemplate. But in a short poem like 'I Wandered Lonely as a Cloud' such awareness underpins the experience. In 'Tintern Abbey' Wordsworth describes having learned from nature how to achieve a meditative state similar to the conclusion of the daffodils poem that he describes as

>   that serene and blessed mood
> In which the affections gently lead us on,

Until, the breath of this corporeal frame,
And even the motion of our human blood
Almost suspended, we are laid asleep
In body, and become a living soul:
While with an eye made quiet by the power
Of harmony, and the deep power of joy,
We see into the life of things. (42–50)

Some of Wordsworth's thinking here is reminiscent of Hartley's associationism—particularly his ideas about the way complex pleasures derived from seeing landscapes may recur by 'reviewing' them in the mind—but it certainly also has an emphasis on a kind of intuitive cognition that seems quasi-mystical and that anticipates American Transcendentalists such as Ralph Waldo Emerson and Henry David Thoreau (see Chapter 5). Wordsworth's use of the word *things* here is not carelessly general—he literally means things, as in non-human objects that the 'living soul' in this state apprehends as sharing the same vitality. Moreover, in the Preface to *Lyrical Ballads* he writes that 'my habits of meditation have so formed my feelings, as that my descriptions of such objects as strongly excite those feelings, will be found to carry along with them a *purpose*' (*LBRW* 393). In a sense, his purpose is to help his readers develop similar habits by reading poetry and learning to perceive the interconnectedness of all people and things. The skill, if it may be so termed, required to impart such learning is fundamentally a refined act of the imagination. And this is why a poet is best suited for the job of helping us understand this deeper truth.

Wordsworth sees the imagination and the physical senses working in mutual cooperation: in 'Tintern Abbey' he celebrates 'the mighty world / Of eye and ear, both what they half create, / And what perceive' (106–8). So, at least half of what we perceive is objective reality, but the other half is created by our subjective imagination. And this brings us to another feature of Wordsworth's poetry that has become common in understanding Romanticism—the prioritizing and foregrounding of subjectivity. Wordsworth became more interested in lyric poetry while he, Dorothy Wordsworth, and Coleridge were in Germany; there Coleridge immersed himself in German Enlightenment philosophy that would define his thinking for the rest of his career. It is uncertain the extent to which Wordsworth read these philosophers, but it is safe to assume that Coleridge, who loved nothing more than imparting his knowledge through conversation, shared many of these ideas with Wordsworth. One German thinker who may be particularly helpful in assessing the depth of 'I Wandered Lonely as a Cloud' is Johann Gottlieb Fichte (1762–1814), who proposed a model of subjectivity—*das Ich* ('the I')—that is not unlike the Freudian 'ego.' The refined act of the imagination described above, which Wordsworth wishes to describe to his readers, is similar to what Fichte called the state of *Anschauung*, which literally means sense-perception, but which, in Romantic thought, is the direct intuition or apprehension of knowledge without the prior intervention of reason in interpreting it. A notebook entry of 1801 reveals that Coleridge used Wordsworth's 'Tintern Abbey'— particularly the line 'We see into the *Life* of Things' (Coleridge's emphasis)—as a way of understanding Fichte's *Anschauung*, a process by which 'the I' understands itself as existing in the act of thinking, but also that it is distinct from that which it contemplates (Stempel 375). In Fichte, this is a kind of passiveness in which the ego forgets itself, a kind of intuition that is, in Daniel Stempel's words, 'the lowest level of imagination' but that 'functions on all levels' up to the 'highest synthesis of poetic and philosophic thought' (373).

In Wordsworth the subjectivity of the lyric speaker/poet is both the *raison d'être* and the *modus operandi*. This subjectivity complicates simple poems such as 'I Wandered Lonely as a Cloud' and underlies more sophisticated poems such as 'Tintern Abbey' or the 'Intimations Ode'—and especially *The Prelude*— through the refraction of the intuitive 'I' into poetic expression (metaphor, simile, symbolism, etc.). The daffodils poem dramatizes the Fichtean thought experiment that Coleridge works out in his notebook using 'Tintern Abbey': the speaker/poet perceives the daffodils (and a 'host' of other contingencies); he intuits, without thinking, a distinction between himself as subject and the daffodils as object—and this intuition is pleasure. But he does not recognize the *value* of the experience until later. At the end of the poem, he literally re-views the daffodils, but they are no longer objective, or outside of the self; instead, they are manifestations of thought in the subjectivity of the speaker/poet and therefore of the speaker/poet himself. Subjectivity occurs when the thinker and the thought are one in the act of thinking. This is the climax as well as the lesson of the poem. The value of the experience comes later as a purely subjective, internal process. Wordsworth is interested in epistemological process and in modeling a response to the world that his readers may replicate in responding to the verse. The poetry contains moments of imaginative visitation—intense perceptions that are peculiar to the poet. His job, then, is to convey those experiences and insights so that the ordinary reader may experience the pleasure and the moral benefit of them. So, the experience of reading the poetry conveys essentially the same benefits for the reader as the original experiences and perceptions did for the poet. As Wordsworth explained to Coleridge, poetry should 'remind men of their knowledge, as it lurks inoperative and unvalued in their own minds, [rather than] attempt to convey recondite or refined truths' (*Middle Years* 2: 238).

Nature and Memory

Dealing with the 'Daffodils,' then, is serious business for Wordsworth—especially when we consider how its emphasis on memory, imagination, and poetic creativity coincides with the composition of *The Prelude*. James A. Butler has called the poem 'a miniature Prelude' (51). Most pertinent to our discussion here is the notion Wordsworth introduces in Book XI of 'spots of time,' impressive moments from our past that are colored in our memory by an awareness of the mind's sublime power and that 'retain / A renovating Virtue' (11.258–60). Much like he does in 'Tintern Abbey,' Wordsworth explains that memory has the power to restore, to repair, and to renovate one's spirit; but here he places less emphasis on Nature's role in this process and more on the mind's internal activity:

> This efficacious spirit chiefly lurks
> Among those passages of life in which
> We have had deepest feeling that the mind
> Is lord and master, and that outward sense
> Is but the obedient servant of her will. (11.269–73)

Since this passage comes near the end of *The Prelude*, it appears in the context of formulating a resolution to the problems developed up to this point: after suffering what he considers to be an impairment of his mind, he realizes that his past experiences have helped him to recover the imaginative power he frequently demonstrates in his other poetry—particularly in poems such as 'Tintern Abbey' or 'I Wandered Lonely as a Cloud.' *The Prelude* is about how he gained that power, how he lost it, and how he recovered it. After a moment of crisis, he finds himself revitalized in having arrived at self-fulfillment. He has become the poet of the 'Daffodils.' In Book XI, Wordsworth has brought his poem up to date in terms of that self-actualization; just before introducing the 'spots of time,' Wordsworth writes that he has recovered from empiricism, the 'tyranny' of the senses, in favor of the transcendent (11.180):

> I had felt
> Too forcibly, too early in my life,
> Visitings of imaginative power
> For this to last: I shook the habit off
> Entirely and for ever, and again
> In Nature's presence stood, as I stand now,
> A sensitive, and a creative soul. (11.251–7)

Thinking about this passage in terms of the daffodils and of the Enlightenment (see Chapter 1), we see Wordsworth grappling with the competing claims of rationalism and empiricism, as Kant does, but with different results (although the influence of both on the American Transcendentalists would seem to suggest some similarity). Like Kant, though, Wordsworth accepts transcendental knowledge in the sense that the mind is capable of *a priori* knowledge, or knowledge independent of experience. Wordsworth attributes this transcendence to Nature, the 'efficacious spirit' that convinces him that 'the mind / Is lord and master.' It sounds like rationalism in the pre-eminence it places on the mind, but it has a mystical relationship to Nature that *The Prelude* explores without systematizing, and that has become Wordsworth's trademark.

Re-Vision and Revision

Returning to the daffodils, we should remember that, in a poem made public especially, Wordsworth would be concerned with connecting to his readers, so we might think about the way he revised his work presumably with the intention of making the poetry do so more effectively. So, eight years after its first publication, 'I Wandered Lonely as a Cloud' reappears in a revised form in his 1815 collection *Poems by William Wordsworth*. Here, the poem again is untitled but is now numbered 13 in a series of 33 'Poems of the Imagination' that opens with the fragment 'There was a boy,' an excerpt from *The Prelude*, and concludes with 'Tintern Abbey.' Reading the daffodils poem in this context alone suggests immediate differences in how to approach the poem—particularly in its new association with the earlier 'Tintern Abbey.' Wordsworth made a few changes in word choice, but the major difference is the insertion of a new stanza after the first one, which ends with the daffodils 'Fluttering and dancing in the breeze' (instead of the original sixth line 'Ten thousand dancing in the breeze'). The new stanza reads as follows:

> Continuous as the stars that shine
> And twinkle on the milky way,
> They stretched in never-ending line
> Along the margin of a bay:
> Ten thousand saw I at a glance,
> Tossing their heads in sprightly dance.

Two questions come to mind immediately: why might Wordsworth have added this stanza? Does it improve the poem? This stanza certainly adds a surprising element to the figurative language of the poem and possibly therefore a surprising effect: David Perkins asserts that the 'odd association' between the daffodils and outer space suggests to the reader 'feelings of sublimity and infinitude' that 'seem strangely inappropriate to this scene of lake and flowers' (194). The new classification of the poem among 'Poems of the Imagination' suggests that the poet sees this poem as expressing something more than a 'mood' of his 'own mind' and that its being of the imagination is a kind of elevation in status, particularly as this series follows a lighter series of 'Poems of the Fancy.' Prior to the nineteenth century, the terms *fancy* and *imagination* largely were synonymous, but Wordsworth and Coleridge made clear distinctions between the two. Obviously, Wordsworth creates two categories, 'Poems of the Fancy' and 'Poems of the Imagination'; Coleridge, in Chapter 13 of his *Biographia Literaria*, explains his view that the imagination is essentially (and powerfully) creative while the fancy is merely (and randomly) associative. While he was not as dismissive of fancy as Coleridge was, Wordsworth certainly agreed that the imagination was a higher faculty than fancy and says so explicitly in the 1815 Preface that *imagination* is 'a word of higher import, denoting operations of the mind upon those objects, and processes of creation or of composition' (*MW* 631).

The addition of the new stanza to 'I Wandered Lonely as a Cloud' may be considered, then, in this light: Wordsworth wanted to give the poem more of an imaginative impulse that accords with its graduation from 'Moods of My Own Mind' to 'Poems of the Imagination.' The new series in 1815 ends with 'Tintern Abbey' and its celebration of the 'sense sublime,' so the new stanza adds language to the poem that evokes the sublime. For instance, the simile that begins the new stanza is not only astonishing but seems intended to stagger the imagination in the same manner as the sublime does. Moreover, the image of the daffodils stretching 'in never-ending line / Along the margin of a bay' not only expands the lake from the first stanza into a hypothetical bay but also extends the metaphor to hyperbole, making the imagined bay also 'never-ending' in its immensity. Matthew C. Brennan suggests that the poem be read as 'an experience of the *sublime*,' emphasizing the way this stanza in particular 'imagines [the daffodils] as infinite' (141). Indeed, in his discussion of the imagination in the Preface to the 1815 collected works, Wordsworth asserts that the imagination is nothing less than 'a sublime consciousness of the soul in her own mighty and almost divine powers' (*MW* 633). This definition of the soul might then correspond with the power that displays itself in the final stanza of the poem, which remains unchanged. Wordsworth, however, does add a curious footnote to the line 'They flash upon that inward eye': having explained in the Preface that the first group of poems following 'There was a boy,' and including the daffodils, 'exhibit the faculty [imagination] exerting itself upon various objects of the external universe,' Wordsworth qualifies this in relation to 'I Wandered Lonely as a Cloud.' He writes in the footnote, 'The subject of these Stanzas is rather an elementary feeling and simple impression . . . upon the imaginative faculty, than an *exertion* of it.' Wordsworth thus explains a difference between this poem and those that immediately precede it, including such poems as 'Nutting,' 'She Was a Phantom of Delight,' 'Three Years She Grew,' 'A Slumber Did My Spirit Seal,' and 'Goody Blake and Harry Gill.' These poems presumably show the 'exertion' of the imagination, whereas the daffodils poem shows the imagination in reception. One might wonder, then, why he added the new stanza, which, more than the original stanzas do, displays the imagination in exertion. For Coleridge one of Wordsworth's faults as a poet was his tendency to employ 'thoughts and images too great for the subject' (*Biographia* 2: 136). Perhaps this poem works better as one of the 'Moods of My Own Mind' than as one of the 'Poems of the Imagination.'

Readers should always examine poets' attempts to clarify, to refine, or to expand with a critical eye—especially in the cases of Wordsworth and Coleridge. Wordsworth's 'I Wandered Lonely as a Cloud' thus provides a case study in reading Wordsworth, for it raises many of the issues that pertain to reading any one of his poems. Wordsworth's characteristic simplicity of diction and form should never be mistaken for simplicity of intent or simplicity of thought, for his poetry is almost always engaging, whether directly or obliquely, philosophical, epistemological, social, and aesthetic ideas. And because of his longevity, Wordsworth has left us with multiple—often competing—versions of his work, giving us the opportunity as readers to evaluate for ourselves which versions suit our own various interests, concerns, and tastes. The poems of 'the great decade,' 1798 to 1807, will continue to raise these questions and afford these opportunities.

FOR FURTHER STUDY

1. 'I Wandered Lonely as a Cloud' is based on an experience that Dorothy Wordsworth records in her *Grasmere Journal* for April 15, 1802 (84–5, *MW* 714). Compare Dorothy Wordsworth's account with the poem: you will notice several borrowings but resist the impulse to accuse Wordsworth of plundering his sister's writing; consider, instead, his adaptation of the shared experience to his poetic purposes and Dorothy Wordsworth's autonomy as a writer in her own right.

SECTION TWO: 'THE RUINED COTTAGE'

'THE STRONG CREATIVE POWER OF HUMAN PASSION'

'I Wandered Lonely as a Cloud' has provided an opportunity to establish some key concepts and strategies for reading Wordsworth's poetry. Next, I want to offer a framework for reading 'the great decade' by going back to the start of the collaboration between Wordsworth and Coleridge and working chronologically through exemplary poems from the first and second editions of *Lyrical Ballads*, finally coming full circle with the 1807 *Poems, in Two Volumes*, in which the daffodils poem first appeared. This chapter then concludes with Wordsworth's 'Intimations Ode,' which also closed the 1807 volume. The emphasis throughout will be on the lyrical and narrative strains in Wordsworth's poetry.

The best poem for beginning that study is one that most readers over the past 200 years would not have recognized as a stand-alone work. Now one of Wordsworth's most commonly anthologized poems, 'The Ruined Cottage' did not appear in print as such until Jonathan Wordsworth published his edition of it in 1969. The bulk of the poem first appeared as a section from the first book of a longer poem *The Excursion*, published in 1814. But Coleridge regretted its inclusion in *The Excursion* and felt that it should have stood alone as 'one of the most beautiful poems in the language' (*Specimens* 2: 69). Wordsworth began writing it in 1797 and revised it according to feedback from Coleridge in 1798. Because of Coleridge's influence on the poem and because it derives from the period scholars call the *annus mirabilis*, 'The Ruined Cottage' usefully constructs a way of reading the *Lyrical Ballads*. So, even though Wordsworth would continue to revise the poem over the years, readers may read the 1798 version that now is widely available in editions of Wordsworth such as Gill's *Major Works* and in anthologies such as the *Norton Anthology of English Literature*.

Arguably his first great poem, 'The Ruined Cottage' is a narrative that concerns a woman named Margaret, who has lived and died in the 'ruined cottage.' Because of a severely debilitated economy, her husband, Robert, formerly a hard-working weaver, finds he is unable to provide for the family and, deserting them, enlists as a soldier. He never returns, and Margaret, in her despair, grows neglectful of her children and her home, finally dying in a dilapidated weed-infested house that had once been an idyllic domestic scene of nurturing and thriving. But this is only the narrative core of the poem. As we will see, one of the fundamental characteristics of *Lyrical Ballads* is that Wordsworth and Coleridge are interested in the intersections between poetic insight and rustic storytelling and the resulting complexities of perspective—lyrical, narrative, and social. 'The Ruined Cottage' thus is similar to many of the poems from this period and brings to the fore many of the contextual and poetic issues raised in our first two chapters: it is a humanitarian poem with a rural setting; it is a narrative that develops through the interaction between a speaker and another character who tells the story—a device that allows Wordsworth to impart a social lesson regarding the conditions of the poor as well as a more mystical one involving harmony with the natural world and coming to terms with the transience of mortality. It concerns a 'forsaken woman' who goes mad, and it reveals the poet's interest in the psychology of feeling, suffering, and sympathy. The narrative frame allows Wordsworth to explore Margaret's suffering as well as the hearer's / reader's response to it and, without denying the injustice of the poor woman's condition, to suggest the spiritual and moral value in participating in the poetic representation of her sorrows.

The poem has two narrators and thus two frames, an outer-frame and an inner-frame, with Margaret's story contained within both: the first is an outer-narrator we might call the poet-speaker who introduces us to the second, an inner-narrator who tells Margaret's story. The outer-frame opens with poetic description that sets a mood not unlike the opening of Coleridge's 'Eolian Harp' and does not necessarily seem much like the beginning of a story. But 'the dreaming man' who enjoys the scene described in the first 18-and-a-half lines, we learn, is hypothetical: it is 'Pleasant to him'—the third-person subject rather than the first-person subject we might expect—who reclines on 'the soft cool grass.' The speaker of the poem imposes himself upon the poem in unpleasant contrast to the opening—'Other lot was mine,' he tells us and then describes himself slogging across a slippery 'bare wide Common,' collapsing on 'the brown earth' too weary to swat away the annoying insects. Wordsworth thus disrupts the pastoral idyll of the first verse-paragraph to offer instead what we might call realistic detail. So, the narrative frame is even more complicated by the opening of the poem. With such a surprising contrast, Wordsworth clearly is experimenting with narrative.

The poet-speaker rises and finds among the trees 'a ruined house, four naked walls / That stared upon each other' and there near the door he sees the old pedlar Armytage, whom the speaker happily recognizes. The name *Armytage* suggests *hermitage*— a somewhat unusual English surname from the Greek *eremos* meaning 'solitary.' The pedlar directs the poet-speaker to a hidden garden plot defiled by weeds, a 'cheerless spot' where Armytage begins the tale and the poet-speaker rests to listen. In the 1798 version of the poem the pedlar reminds the poet of the devastating effects of two bad harvests and 'the plague of war' that occurred 'some ten years gone,' which sets the poem a few years prior to its composition and thus refers to the American war for independence—although the economic circumstances apply more accurately to the conditions of 1794–1795, as the revised timeline for this episode in *The Excursion* affirms ('Not twenty years ago'). Wordsworth needed this distance in order to draw Margaret's slow pitiful decline as she waits for Robert's return. Robert never does return, so the 'ruined cottage' in which they had made their home ultimately represents the abandoned woman's emotional and physical decay. The house's condition, then, functions as metonymy for Margaret's because the house is already associated with this particular family's domestic life.

From a broader social perspective, the ruined cottage itself might also work as a metaphor for the condition of the rural poor suffering from the devastating economic circumstances of the time, a major component of Wordsworth's context as we have already seen. Since Jerome McGann's groundbreaking work *The Romantic Ideology* (1983), critics have studied ways in which poems such as 'The Ruined Cottage' actually attempt, in McGann's words, 'to occlude and disguise their own involve-ment in a certain nexus of historical relations' by not explicitly indicting social and political customs and institutions responsi-ble for such deplorable conditions (82). This particular poem, McGann argues, works to 'elide' the specific examples and their particular causes 'from our memories' (83). The trajectory of the poem enacts the displacement of Wordsworth's political outrage from earlier in the decade (see Chapter 1) to 'a sense of shame and humility' and 'an overflow of sympathy and love for the sufferer' (85). Even though this version of the poem remained unpublished, Wordsworth generally does want his reader to care about the poor and wants his reader to think about questions of mortality and the value of all human life, as his repurposing of this text for *The Excursion* (and thus for his epic project, *The Recluse*) shows. As we have seen in Chapter 1, Wordsworth has inherited the legacy of Sensibility and uses sympathy as one of his poetic tools. But he also wants to make his reader think as well as feel, believing that the thinking will leave a more lasting impression than the feeling. The relationship between the poet-speaker and the pedlar is an example of how Wordsworth tries to accomplish this. So, it is worth considering why Wordsworth revised the poem so that Margaret's story is told not by the poet but by the rustic pedlar, who seems to have a mystical insight that the poet-speaker has only begun to appreciate. When Armytage speaks, he opens his portion of the poem with the solemn reflection that

> we die, my Friend,
> Nor we alone, but that which each man loved
> And prized in his peculiar nook of earth
> Dies with him or is changed, and very soon
> Even of the good is no memorial left. (69–72)

These lines certainly accord with the setting in which the two men interact—although the poet-speaker never speaks directly to the pedlar; he only listens and responds with emotion at the end.

But the pedlar seems aware that his companion is a poet because he addresses the power of poets to find sympathy with the natural world and to speak 'with a voice / Obedient to the strong creative power / Of human passion' (77–9). The pedlar acts as the Wordsworthian teacher to the poet-speaker. The function of the pedlar in the poem is a Wordsworthian innovation: the framing structure of the narrative from poet to pedlar to tale gives Wordsworth the opportunity to model how sympathetic response becomes intellectual reflection and ultimately spiritual recognition in oneself. Over the course of the poem, the pedlar teaches the poet how to transform his response into something transcendent, thus modeling the way for the reader to experience and value the process of reading.

These lessons are difficult ones. The first part of the poem ends with the pedlar suggesting that grief is 'the weakness of humanity' turning away from 'natural wisdom' and 'natural comfort' (194–6). On the one hand, the pedlar is concerned that stories of others' suffering not be merely for entertainment; on the other, he tells his 'tale of silent suffering' with an 'easy chearfulness' that defies tears (233, 201). The pedlar begins to seem stoically inhuman.

We might compare the interaction between the pedlar and the poet-speaker to that between Coleridge's 'Ancyent Marinere' and the wedding guest, from the poem Coleridge was writing with Wordsworth's advice at around the same time. The pedlar, however, has no supernatural power to hold the listener in thrall, only the power of language: 'He had rehearsed / Her homely tale with such familiar power . . . that the things of which he spake / Seemed present' (208–12). But why tell a story of woe without inspiring pity? The pedlar, and probably Wordsworth, does not want this to be a poem of Sensibility where feeling is the main object. Nor does he want to tell a remarkable story: Margaret's story is common, 'By moving accidents uncharacter'd,' that is, having no particularly interesting events, and thus will not satisfy 'the grosser sense' of a listener (reader) 'who does not think' (234–6). Wordsworth performs a similar maneuver in 'Simon Lee,' from *Lyrical Ballads*, although he does so more pointedly, as we will see.

Like many of the poems in *Lyrical Ballads*, 'The Ruined Cottage' bears the influence of Cowper's 'Crazy Kate' passage from *The Task* (1785) in its portrayal of the 'forsaken woman' (the phrase comes from Wordsworth's 'Complaint of the Forsaken Indian Woman'). In Cowper's passage, Kate's madness apparently derives from her 'delusive' fancy that imagines her lover's return and, as Cowper implies, from her frustrated sexual desire for 'transports she was not to know.' Wordsworth's description of Margaret's hope and longing is similar but more subtle: she sits outside on a bench for hours while she gazes off 'in the distance, shaping things / Which made her heart beat quick' (456–7). Wordsworth heightens the pathos with the tragic implication that it is this fervent hope that finally kills her. And once her children are dead (possibly from neglect) she succumbs herself. An early draft of the poem ends here: 'In sickness she remained, and here she died, / Last human tenant of these ruined walls' (491–2). But Wordsworth added the pedlar's final words to the emotionally moved poet-speaker. Readers likely will find the pedlar's resolution difficult to accept and will share instead the poet-speaker's sympathetic response. This is the challenge of the poem: Wordsworth replaces the 'unprofitable bindweed' that subdues the rose (314–17) with 'the high spear grass'; this 'image of tranquility' dispels the old man's own 'uneasy thoughts' (514–19). This leads him to conclude that

> all the grief
> The passing shows of being leave behind,
> Appeared an idle dream that could not live
> Where meditation was. I turned away,
> And walked along my road in happiness. (521–5)

Is this stoicism? Or is it the kind of philosophical optimism that Voltaire parodies in *Candide*? Is it Christian resignation to the will of providence? (There is a stoic strain in Wordsworth: a later poem 'Laodamia,' written in 1814, would reflect a tension between stoic resignation and passionate grief.) Again, we might recall the similarly framed 'Rime of the Ancyent Marinere' from *Lyrical Ballads*: the pedlar may be a counterpart of the mariner, both seeming to offer a moral that requires deeper inspection. Is it possible that, like the mariner, the pedlar is oblivious to the deeper implications of the story he tells? In Coleridge's poem, the wedding guest, the listener, rises the next day 'a sadder and a wiser man,' a response suggesting he has taken away from the mariner's tale something quite different than the mariner's stated lesson; in Wordsworth's poem, the poet-speaker closes the frame without comment on the pedlar's words and is 'admonished' only by the lateness of the hour. The wedding guest in Coleridge's poem turns away from the social ceremony, disturbed by the experience; the poet-speaker and the pedlar walk together to 'A rustic inn, our evening-resting place' and rejoin society.

Since Coleridge's 'Rime of the Ancyent Marinere' is the lead poem in the 1798 *Lyrical Ballads*, such comparisons lead to fruitful consideration of the famous collaboration between the two poets. Like the daffodils poem, 'The Ruined Cottage' provides an exemplar of how to study the textual issues regarding the reading of Wordsworth's poetry. Editors have studied the multiple manuscripts of the poem and several revisions to this section of *The Excursion*. Wordsworth developed from an early draft of 'The Ruined Cottage' a separate poem about the pedlar's life and experiences and then combined the two in *The Excursion*. A few years before his death, Wordsworth revised this section of *The Excursion* one final time and gave the pedlar's conclusion a more specifically Christian theme as Margaret 'learned, with soul / Fixed on the Cross, that consolation springs / From sources deeper far than deepest pain.' This later version contrasts sharply with the pedlar's assertion in the 1799 version that 'She sleeps in the calm earth, and peace is here.' Today's readers may consider which they prefer. James Butler's edition for The Cornell Wordsworth and Jonathan Wordsworth's *The Music of Humanity* are excellent sources for more on the textual history. John Rieder studies how these multiple revisions and changes to the frames affect interpretation of the poem.

FOR FURTHER STUDY

1. Why not make the pedlar, Armytage, the primary narrator of the poem? Or make the poet-speaker the narrator of Margaret's story? What effect do the three narrative layers have on the reader's experience of the poem?
2. Readers may find interesting comparisons between 'The Ruined Cottage,' 'The Female Vagrant,' and 'The Complaint of the Forsaken Indian Woman,' both from *Lyrical Ballads*, and his later poem *The White Doe of Rylstone* (1815), particularly in the poet's portrayal of the abandoned woman character.
3. Compare 'The Ruined Cottage' with a similar portrayal of the destruction of a rural family in 'Michael' (see below).

SECTION THREE: READING *LYRICAL BALLADS*

As we have seen in the first two chapters, the collaboration between Wordsworth and Coleridge was born of frustration and discontent with literary conventions of the late eighteenth century—as well as of creative excitement and friendship among Wordsworth, Coleridge, and Dorothy Wordsworth. The previous chapter discussed the stylistically experimental nature of the project, so here we will begin to look at specific examples of the ways that paying attention to style and form can help readers get the most out of these poems. Of particular importance is Wordsworth's experimentation with narrative within the poetic form. By deploying complicated narrative devices, such as frames and dialogues, within deceptively simple poems of feeling, he is able to further the aesthetic and ethical project of his work.

First off, it is worth considering the sequence of the poems in the volume: after the 'Advertisement,' written by Wordsworth, the volume opens with 'The Rime of the Ancyent Marinere,' which does not immediately challenge the claims Wordsworth makes in the 'Advertisement.' It starts simply enough. As the poem proceeds, however, the Marinere asserts a supernatural hold on his auditor, the wedding guest, and begins his bizarre tale of nightmarish guilt and penance. The relationship of Coleridge's poem to the rest of *Lyrical Ballads* is a fascinating subject for readers to consider. Both poets expressed some concern that it might not fit well with the other poems, and it certainly received its share of criticism: while conceding some brilliant touches, for example, both Robert Southey, a mutual friend, and critic Charles Burney attacked it, the former calling it 'a poem of little merit' and the latter describing it as 'the strangest story of a cock and a bull that we ever saw on paper' (*LBRW* 354, 359). But without getting too deep into the poem's unfathomable mysteries, suffice it to say that the 'Ancyent Marinere' does introduce the complex relationship between narrative, narrator, and poetic ambiguity that pervades the rest of the volume. For example, the reader soon enough realizes that, instead of the traditional balladeer-as-narrator, this ballad is primarily told by a character-narrator who appears to be operating under supernatural agency; and as suggested by the comparison with 'The Ruined Cottage' above, the lesson articulated by the mariner and the lesson imparted to the wedding guest appear to be incongruous with one another. By the end of 'The Rime of the Ancyent Marinere,' the insightful reader is aware that the concept of a 'lyrical ballad' allows for considerable irony and provocative ambiguity. Complexities abound in what appear on the surface to be fairly simple narrative poems.

After the aesthetic shock of 'The Rime of the Ancyent Marinere' the reader of *Lyrical Ballads* as a book finds him or herself in more familiar terrain with Coleridge's 'The Foster-Mother's Tale' and Wordsworth's 'Lines Left upon a Seat in a Yew-Tree.' In Coleridge's 'Dramatic Fragment,' extracted from his tragedy *Osorio*, two characters engage in a dialogue regarding the fate of an iconoclastic young man who, having grown up in a manner like that proposed by Rousseau—that is, among nature with little influence from civilization until adulthood—ultimately escapes persecution for his 'heretical and lawless talk' by fleeing to the New World, where he 'lived and died among the savage men.' This fragment forms a pair with Wordsworth's 'Lines Left upon a Seat in a Yew-Tree,' a poem that tells of another unconventional figure who escapes society for solitude in nature. So, here is a portrait of the Wordsworthian solitary who appears so often in his work. But it is a warning against solitude as an excuse for self-absorption and misanthropy: the person described here feeds his soul 'with the food of pride' and finds in the beauty of nature only 'An emblem of his own unfruitful life' (20, 28). The poem concludes with the admonition that those 'whose heart[s] the holy forms / Of young imagination have kept pure' not allow themselves to be corrupted by pride (44–5). Here begins, too, the volume's insistent theme of thought arising from experience and feeling: 'he, who feels contempt / For any living thing, hath faculties / Which he has never used' (48–50). Feeling and thinking, as we have seen, must cooperate properly in harmony with one another through a concerted harmony with nature. Throughout *Lyrical Ballads* Wordsworth reminds his readers that they should think about what they are reading and learn therefore 'that true knowledge leads to love' (55). This is the first poem in the volume to explicitly express the Wordsworthian *philia* that will become his signature. More specifically, Wordsworth wants to write poetry that will confer a moral benefit upon the reader by imparting the skills through which we might improve our abilities to experience and perceive the world. *The Prelude* explores how the poet arrives at this confidence, but the poems of 'the great decade' show him putting it

into practice and doing so in relation to an audience, a public
that he expects to build.

As I have written, the most original aspect of *Lyrical Ballads*
is the way the poems in it challenge the reader's expectations for
poetry—but not only stylistic expectations concerning diction,
form, and genre. These poems repeatedly dare the reader to turn
away from the subjects they describe. 'Lines Left upon a Seat in
a Yew-Tree' does so explicitly in its opening lines:

> —Nay, Traveller! Rest. This lonely yew-tree stands
> Far from all human dwelling: what if here
> No sparkling rivulet spread the verdant herb;
> What if these barren boughs the bee not loves[?] (1–4)

Since the first two poems are by Coleridge, these lines serve as
Wordsworth's first poetic address to the reader, whom the poet
figures metaphorically as a traveler who might not stop here and
thus pass on to the next poem (Coleridge's 'The Nightingale').
The rhetorical questions make the point that this is not a par-
ticularly attractive spot to rest because it is not picturesque.
Wordsworth's use of the conventional poeticisms 'sparkling riv-
ulet' and 'verdant herb' suggest the influence of aesthetic theory
of the picturesque developed by William Gilpin. In contrast to
Edmund Burke's aesthetic distinctions in natural scenery between
the sublime, which inspires awe or even terror, and the beautiful,
which inspires love, Gilpin described the picturesque as scenery
that pleases because it appears to be suitable for a painting or a
scene that actually seems composed according to the principles
of landscape painting—as we might say, 'pretty as a picture.'
Wordsworth's description of how the scene does *not* appear
emphasizes the unimpressive quality of this particular spot. In
this way, his first address to the reader reinforces the claims and
concerns of his 'Advertisement,' that the style and substance of
his poems may not seem to his readers to be appropriate for
poetry. But he suggests that, should the traveler stop here, he or she
will find other attractions: 'Yet, if the wind breathe soft, the curl-
ing waves, / That break against the shore, shall lull thy mind / By
one soft impulse saved from vacancy' (5–7). Wordsworth prefig-
ures the idea that he will reassert throughout, culminating at
the end of the volume in 'Expostulation and Reply,' 'The Tables

Turned,' and 'Tintern Abbey'—the 'One impulse from a vernal wood' that teaches more about human morality than the philosophers can do. The yew-tree affords a Wordsworthian experience where only 'one soft impulse,' one sensation, shall soothe the traveler's mind and make it receptive to the scene; by extension, the reader's mind is prepared for the narrative of the misanthrope in the next verse-paragraph and then the moral lesson in the poem's third and final section. The yew-tree holds the 'monument' left by the proud man who made the seat of its trunk and by the poet who has written the lines left there; poet must actively involve the traveler / reader in the life and sensations described in order for the moral to have any validity. As the poems challenge the reader to think, Wordsworth expects that the poems also will inspire the requisite feelings in his reader necessary to validate the ideas.

Simon Lee: 'Perhaps a Tale You'll Make It'

Readers should keep in mind that the original 1798 volume was called *Lyrical Ballads, with a Few Other Poems*. Neither Wordsworth nor Coleridge ever specified which poems are 'lyrical ballads' and which are the 'other poems,' but I think we can assume that the 'lyrical ballads' are those that demonstrate the most sophisticated play on the traditions of lyric and ballad; as we saw in Chapter 2, this generic play is an important part of reading Wordsworth. One of the more innovative poems from *Lyrical Ballads* and, in my opinion, the most perfect 'lyrical ballad' is 'Simon Lee, the Old Huntsman with an Incident in which He Was Concerned.' This poem begins as a ballad in the strain of the rustic and antiquarian poetry that was popular in the second half of the eighteenth century, such as Percy's *Reliques* (1765) or Robert Burns's *Tam o' Shanter* (1791). And, as Robert Mayo has shown, the subject would have been familiar to readers of newspapers and magazines of the day, which frequently depicted the hardships of the poor. Wordsworth plays upon his readers' familiarity with such poetry, as Paul Sheats points out, 'to elicit a stock response' that the poet then proceeds to undermine in order to make a stronger point about the hardships of the poor (189). Wordsworth presents a portrait of an elderly huntsman by juxtaposing almost comic descriptions of his decline—'And, though he has but one eye left, / His cheek is like a cherry'

59

(15–16)—with contrasting descriptions of the former glories of his younger days, his 'hunting feats,' and the times when 'He all the country could outrun, / Could leave both man and horse behind' (25, 41–2). The augmented, or feminine, rhymes and the speaker's gossipy, familiar tone contribute to the disorienting, almost bathetic quality of the description. After four eight-line stanzas, the speaker informs the reader of the pathos of Simon's situation: age and infirmity have left his body twisted 'half awry' so that his elderly wife, Ruth, must do most of the work to earn what little they can from their 'scrap of land' (34, 61).

The diction Wordsworth employs to describe Simon's decline, such as in the line 'His ancles they are swoln and thick' (35), likely is the kind that he refers to in the 1798 'Advertisement' to *Lyrical Ballads*, where he warns his readers that they may find some phrases distasteful and 'not of sufficient dignity' (*LBRW* 21). Although part of his experiment with poetic diction, the use of such 'low' and 'familiar' phrases has a political dimension, as noted earlier. Wordsworth subtly suggests that the couple's situation has been made worse by Parliament's Enclosure Acts, which allowed landowners to fence off common land that had previously been open to anyone to cultivate; thus Simon and his wife likely would have had to rely entirely on charity had they not had their own tiny plot of land. But this land, he reminds us, is hardly enough, especially when the tenants are too old to work and, indeed, are on the verge of death.

The reader thus far expects a story from the ballad, but Wordsworth's speaker interrupts with a surprising address to his 'gentle reader' who has waited 'patiently' for 'Some tale [to] be related' (69–72). Echoing the class marker 'gentle' a second time, Wordsworth criticizes the complacent middle- to upper-class readers who might only be interested in a figure such as Simon for their own amusement:

> O reader! had you in your mind
> Such stores as silent thought can bring,
> O gentle reader! you would find
> A tale in every thing. (73–6)

Wordsworth uses these formal expectations to assert that readers ought to care about the poor without the requirement of a remarkable or entertaining narrative. The speaker then enters the poem to describe first-hand the 'incident' alluded to in the title: the younger man finds Simon struggling with an old tree stump and easily severs the root. Simon's tearful gratitude is overwhelming to the speaker; and just as we expect the moral of the poem to be that the young should help the old, Wordsworth refuses to sentimentalize the situation or to suggest such a simple solution to the problems of the poor. Echoing Godwin's *Political Justice*, Wordsworth's 'Simon Lee' finds gratitude on the part of the poor to be deeply troubling because it is based on the unequal distribution of wealth and power and is thus degrading. But the poem is also formally innovative as a 'lyrical ballad' because it seems to be a ballad that tells only a very slight story, privileging instead the speaker's moment of lyrical insight at the end. It is up to the reader finally to create the tale and to discern the lesson.

FOR FURTHER STUDY

1. Compare 'Simon Lee' with 'Old Man Travelling: Animal Tranquillity and Decay, a Sketch' (*LBRW* 105–6). Wordsworth similarly uses poetic conventions to shock the reader's expectations. The speaker presents a poetic sketch in the first 14 lines (implying perhaps a blank-verse sonnet) that the old man's speech may counter in subtle ways. In his 1815 collection Wordsworth deleted the final six lines of 'Old Man Travelling'—what effect does this have on interpreting the poem?

Personating Loquacity: 'The Thorn'

Like 'Simon Lee,' 'The Thorn' experiments with traditional folk storytelling combined with a more sophisticated, ironic position on the part of the poet that we may think of as 'lyrical'—the insight imparted to the reader is not necessarily discernible in the narrative itself. In the 1798 'Advertisement' to *Lyrical Ballads*, Wordsworth advises the reader that the narrator, or speaker, of the poem 'is not supposed to be spoken in the author's own person: the character of the loquacious narrator will sufficiently shew itself in the course of the story' (*LBRW* 22). Perhaps in response to Robert Southey's complaint about the poem in the *Critical Review* that 'he who personates tiresome loquacity becomes tiresome himself,' Wordsworth, for the second edition of *Lyrical Ballads* (1800), added a lengthy note in which he describes the narrator as a retired 'Captain of a small trading vessel' who has become 'credulous and talkative from indolence' and 'prone to superstition' (*LBRW* 353, 388).

The story of 'The Thorn' involves a woman named Martha Ray who, after being deserted by her lover 22 years prior to the narrator's account, is still seen grieving by the thorn tree and thus is the subject of much curiosity and gossip in the rural community. The narrator's involvement in her story stems only from accidentally encountering her while seeking shelter from the storm. The narrator reports that he has heard the woman was pregnant at the time of her lover's departure and that some villagers speculate that she murdered the baby. The outline of the narrative thus owes much to the ballad 'The Lass of Fair Wone,' translated by William Taylor from the German of Gottfried August Bürger, which appeared in the April 1796 *Monthly Magazine*.

Again, like 'Simon Lee,' the story itself—the ballad—is slight, but it is provocatively grounded in speculations about Martha Ray's sexuality and its potentially dangerous repression. The narrator (like the one in Faulkner's 'A Rose for Emily') speaks for the community with a collective 'we' and, as is often the case with gossip, expresses certainty on the most titillating details: the narrator describes her as wearing 'a scarlet cloak' like the whore of Babylon in Revelation, perhaps indicating the extent to which religious views influence the collective perspective of the community; moreover, Martha Ray, as everyone knows, 'Gave with a maiden's true good will / Her company to Stephen Hill' (117–18)—that is, she had premarital sex with a man who, as it turns out, already was engaged and who subsequently marries another girl. On that 'woful day,' the narrator reports,

A cruel, cruel fire, they say,
Into her bones was sent:
It dried her body like a cinder,
And almost turned her brain to tinder. (129–32)

In the reading of Martha's situation put forth by the community, the bifurcation of body and mind emphasizes how erotic deprivation obviates her natural maternal instincts and perverts her mind with unfulfilled sexual desire. The 'almost' here is potent in its suggestion of repression. It is this presumed desire, then, that actuates the supernatural element the community associates with Martha Ray. When the community decides she must be brought to justice, the narrator reports that, upon their approach, 'for full fifty yards around, / The grass it shook upon the ground' (238–9). What is important here is the community's belief—or possibly only the narrator's belief—in the powerful supernatural expression of Martha's sexuality and how it is associated in their minds with her supposed crime.

In 'The Thorn' gossip and superstition derive from similarly occlusive tendencies in human nature. The poem, furthermore, explores the effect of superstition on the imagination, and on the narrator's ability effectively to see, to interpret, and to explain. The poem consists of 23 eleven-line stanzas, beginning with the narrator's description of the thorn itself in the first four stanzas. The language emphasizes the subjectivity of the narrator's perspective and the way he associates ideas and images; and well before he reveals the story of Martha Ray, Wordsworth's narrator, in the fifth stanza, describes the 'heap of earth o'er grown with moss' next to the thorn as 'like an infant's grave in size' (49, 52)—a telling comparison given the revelations to come, one that seems to accord with Wordsworth's stated intention in the suggestion that the narrator's simile is perhaps subconsciously conditioned by his credulity. As the poem proceeds the narrator imagines his listener's interlocutions, questions, and responses, revealing the limits of his knowledge in replies such as 'I cannot tell; I wish I could' and 'I'll give you the best help I can' (89, 111). The woman's story itself is also marked by equivocations such as "tis said' and 'some say.' The poem thus explores the way this narrator uncritically has absorbed the community's gossip and speculation, and how it has colored his perspective and insidiously damaged a woman's reputation. Or the poem may be more about his mind than her situation and his erotic subconscious; in this light, she may not even truly exist (see Parrish, 'Thorn'). The poem is then further complicated by the difficulty, first proposed by Coleridge, of truly distinguishing between the narrator's account and 'the poet's own imagination' (*Biographia* 2: 50).

Although Coleridge sees this as a flaw, we might see it as a further example of the sophisticated interplay between *lyric* and *ballad*.

FOR FURTHER STUDY

1. 'Goody Blake and Harry Gill' has a narrator similar to the one in 'The Thorn,' and it, like 'Simon Lee' and others in *Lyrical Ballads*, develops a similar lesson about compassion for the rural poor. Although Wordsworth had turned away from Godwin (see Chapter 1), this poem preserves his shared conviction with Godwin that society creates its own criminals; and in this light, the reader should consider the ways in which Wordsworth has adapted the material from his source in Erasmus Darwin's *Zoönomia* (see *LBRW* 59).

Lyrical Ballads and Its Other Forms

The poems that comprise *Lyrical Ballads* offer a range of variations in 'formal engagement.' One of the earliest and one that differs stylistically and politically from the others, 'The Female Vagrant,' is extracted from the longer 'Salisbury Plain' poem that Wordsworth began writing in the summer of 1793 and eventually published as 'Guilt and Sorrow; or, Incidents upon Salisbury Plain' in 1842. It expresses, like 'The Convict,' another poem from *Lyrical Ballads*, the more radical political views Wordsworth held in 1793–1794: in the poem, Wordsworth attacks specifically England's colonialism, its consequent military conflicts and conscription laws that afford the poor relief through military service. Like 'Simon Lee,' the poem also blames Parliamentary Enclosure Acts for enabling the oppression of the rural poor by wealthy landowners. Readers who wish to understand how Wordsworth's political and social views changed as he got older might find it interesting to compare 'The Female Vagrant' with 'Guilt and Sorrow.'

Three other poems from *Lyrical Ballads* with humanitarian themes are what Stephen Maxfield Parrish has identified as belonging to the subgenre of ballad known as 'the complaint' (*Art* 122). Parrish explains that this sort of narrative poem with a speaker who expresses a lament and then concludes with a moral goes back to the old, rustic ballads in Percy's collection. Wordsworth's 'The Mad Mother,' for instance, Parrish suggests, is comparable to 'Lady Anne Bothwell's Lament' from Percy's *Reliques*. While 'The Female Vagrant' hearkens back to conditions earlier in the decade, 'The Last of the Flock' deals with a more specific and up-to-date concern—the predicament of indigent farmers and shepherds who own a small amount of property and who are thus ineligible for assistance according to the poor laws of the day. Counted among the more sentimental poems in *Lyrical Ballads*, it critiques the unfairness of the poor laws that require a shepherd such as the one portrayed in the poem to sell his flock of sheep before he can receive assistance from the parish to save his family from starvation. (We will return to Wordsworth's subversion of the pastoral in his articulation of political and socio-economic concerns in our consideration shortly of 'The Brothers' and 'Michael.')

A most remarkable poem related to humanitarian subjects is Wordsworth's playful 'Idiot Boy,' which readers should approach with more of a sense of humor and fun than perhaps they might expect to be required for a Wordsworth poem. It has the same spirit one finds in Burns's poetry, particularly *Tam o' Shanter*. When read aloud, the rhyme and meter will suggest the great delight Wordsworth took in its composition. Although calling Johnny an 'idiot' seems callous to us as twenty-first-century readers, the poem nonetheless presents what we would call today a mentally challenged young man in a mock-heroic episode, but without sentimentality or pathos and with great respect for his intuitive, imaginative, and joyful experience of life. Wordsworth wants to show how the boy's differentness does not exclude him from the community and certainly does not mitigate the love his mother has for him. As the longest ballad in the volume by Wordsworth, 'The Idiot Boy' may also make for provocative comparison with the other long ballad, Coleridge's 'Rime of the Ancyent Marinere'—particularly in the way both Johnny and the Marinere have imaginative experiences illuminated by moonlight. Johnny, who has never been out at night, is struck by how 'the sun did shine so cold' (460), while the Marinere's blessing of the water-snakes is predicated upon his seeing them by the light of the moon. Both poems also conclude with a provocative undercutting of narrative expectations. As he is delighted by the sights and sounds of nature on his nighttime ride, Johnny's irrationality, Wordsworth shows, is his saving grace. But Wordsworth's emphasis is on Johnny's mother, Betty Foy, and on her love for her son. The poem is playful, even a bit silly, and that may be *its* saving grace.

FOR FURTHER STUDY

1. When a poet chooses a poetic form that is famously associated with another poem he makes a formal allusion to that other poem. For a volume that announces itself as an experiment, why would Wordsworth choose nine-line Spenserian stanza of *The Faerie Queene* from two hundred years previous for 'The Female Vagrant' in *Lyrical Ballads*? Doing so would seem to suggest an intertextual connection with *The Faerie Queene*. Earlier eighteenth-century poets had used the form too, including James Beattie for his poem *The Minstrel; or, the Progress of Genius* (1771) and, surprisingly, Robert Burns for his poem 'The Cotter's Saturday Night' (1786). Does the form lose its association with Spenser when Wordsworth uses it?

2. 'Anecdote for Fathers' and 'We Are Seven' are excellent examples of how feelings may validate and even enhance the ideas behind the poetry. These poems are constructed so that the reader will find it difficult to read against the emotional grain, so how do these poems make their points while playing on the emotional response of the reader? Do these seemingly simple poems do anything to complicate the emotional response? Are these poems 'supposed to be spoken in the author's own person'?

3. David Perkins writes that the 'style and subject of the *Lyrical Ballads* are . . . deliberately calculated to offend and correct the feelings of the sort of person who usually reads poetry— that is, members of the middle and upper classes' (151). How do you see poems from *Lyrical Ballads* doing this?

4. Compare Wordsworth's 'Idiot Boy' with Southey's more serious and sentimental poem 'The Idiot' (*LBRW* 307). Also consider the two in light of Southey's review (*LBRW* 352).

5. Compare 'The Idiot Boy' (1798) and 'The Blind Highland Boy' (1807)—they both involve differently abled children in possibly dangerous scenarios, and each boy has a language of his own. How might the later poem be read against the earlier one?

CONCLUDING *LYRICAL BALLADS*: 'TINTERN ABBEY'

If any poem in *Lyrical Ballads* is one of the 'other poems' it is the conclusion, 'Lines Written a Few Miles above Tintern Abbey, on Revisiting the Banks of the Wye during a Tour, July 13, 1798.' Although the abbey itself does not feature in the poem, it is customary to call the poem simply 'Tintern Abbey,' an irony that continues to engage literary critics with the provocative notion that the poem may be about that which it does not explicitly address (see Chapter 5). It differs from the other Wordsworth poems in *Lyrical Ballads*: it has a loftier diction, it is in blank verse, and it focuses more specifically on the poet himself and his internal experience. As we have seen in Chapter 2, the poem owes a great deal to Coleridge's 'conversation poems' and is not the only poem in *Lyrical Ballads* to follow the general pattern of what M. H. Abrams calls the 'descriptive-meditative poem' (see 'Structure'). So, 'Tintern Abbey' (like Coleridge's 'Eolian Harp,' 'This Lime-Tree Bower My Prison,' 'Frost at Midnight,' 'Fears In Solitude,' and 'The Nightingale') follows basically a three-part structure in which the speaker begins his meditation in a specific place; something there sets the mind and the poem in motion; the poem concludes at the same place, which is changed only because the speaker has. This circular structure permits the 'conversation poem' to have the unity Coleridge believed a poem ought to have, a unity in which all parts mutually support and explain one another. Moreover, 'Tintern Abbey' is a 'conversation poem' because it, like Coleridge's, presents a speaker in relation to an addressee and, through 'conversation,' the speaker seeks to affirm the possibility of something beyond the self. In 'Tintern Abbey' the addressee is the poet's sister, but her presence is not revealed until the poem's final movement.

The important innovation of 'Tintern Abbey'—as it develops from Coleridge's influence—is its celebration of nature combined with a foregrounding of individual perspective, which, as we have seen from the beginning with our consideration of 'I Wandered Lonely as a Cloud,' is essential to Wordsworth's poetics. It expands significantly upon the lyric form to eradicate any distinction between deep feeling and deep thinking; it is therefore a personal dramatization of the effect Wordsworth's poems in *Lyrical Ballads* have suggested throughout. It models a consciousness in communion with nature that unifies feeling and thinking. The lengthy title, moreover, provides important details for reading the poem's dramatization. The title suggests a specific political context—July 13 is the eve of Bastille Day (see Chapter 1)—and a personal context: Wordsworth visited the spot five years earlier after leaving France, the impending Reign of Terror, and his pregnant girlfriend, Annette Vallon. His political allegiances and personal guilt resulted in a confused young man. The opening lines clearly highlight the difference those five intervening five years have made. It is thus also what Mary Jacobus calls a 'revisit poem' (*Tradition* 113). Because of the specificity of place, 'Tintern Abbey' is additionally considered part of the loco-descriptive tradition of poems about particular places. The setting of the poem, therefore, is also important: Tintern Abbey in Wales is a ruined medieval abbey considered to be picturesque, a middle ground between the sublime and beautiful. Again, as the title indicates, Wordsworth's vantage is not the tourist's; it is his own individualized perspective located in the hills above the abbey and the river.

'Tintern Abbey' is a long poem that first-time readers may have difficulty appreciating. But it is a well-organized poem that proceeds almost in an essay-like fashion. Blank-verse poems do not have stanzas; they are organized into verse-paragraphs marked with indentions. 'Tintern Abbey,' then, develops an argument by presenting elements or points in paragraphs, as an essay does. Wordsworth's thesis is that the experience of nature provides an imaginatively, morally, and spiritually sustaining experience that is finally validated by love. It is a poetic *tour de force* that should be read aloud in order to appreciate the enjambments and caesurae that give the verse vitality and variety. Readers may find it helpful to make an outline of the poem paragraph by paragraph, identifying the main point in each of the five sections: lines 1–23, 23–50, 50–8, 59–112, 112–60. Note that, because it is in iambic pentameter and thus each line has ten syllables, paragraphs may break mid-line, the meter continuing to the next paragraph (as in 23, 50, and 112). The paragraphs cohere around points that work toward the conclusion of the poem: the first shows how description of the scene leads to 'thoughts of more deep seclusion'; Wordsworth never describes nature just because it is lovely but because of its effect on the mind and soul. The next paragraph describes the power of memory and the benevolent influence the previous experience has had on him. The short third paragraph briefly calls the previous paragraph's point into doubt before he develops in the fourth paragraph a fuller depiction of his former self, admitting loss in the change but asserting ultimately 'abundant recompence,' emphasizing what he gained (89). He now can hear the 'still, sad music of humanity,' proving that he is now more compassionate, and he has gained 'a sense sublime' that gives him a spiritual awareness of the underlying unity of all things (92, 96).

The final paragraph shifts from his internalized meditation to an acknowledgment of Dorothy's presence with him. Her beloved presence gives the moment a greater profundity and warmth, and Wordsworth introduces her with an echo of Psalm 23.4—'for thou art with me' (115). As he recognizes her as integral to the experience Wordsworth's language moves into the decidedly more religious, becoming literally a prayer. Nature, not the abbey, is his cathedral; he is nature's priest. The poem closes with an evangelium, or gospel, but also with a personal appeal to Dorothy as dear sister and friend to remember him as 'a worshipper of Nature.' As the poem concludes, the reader should consider how her presence enriches the experience and how withholding her presence until this point in the poem helps Wordsworth conclude his poetic essay. She is, after all, seeing this spot for the first time and may represent a younger version of himself from five years ago. Some critics have suggested that he is imposing his perception on her, presenting her like a child even though she is not that much younger than he is. The importance, however, is that her experience, though it may resemble his of five years ago, is different from his now. They share the scene, but not the same perception of it. It is significant that, as he reflects on his own experience, he acknowledges that she has her own deep feelings about the scene—and still there can be connection between them. In this way, the poem is certainly no retreat from social and humanitarian concerns. Wordsworth's presentation of Dorothy may prove the validity of his argument by bringing the poem—and the first edition of *Lyrical Ballads*—to a close with a powerful expression of love and empathy.

FOR FURTHER STUDY

1. The online *Stanford Encyclopedia of Philosophy* provides a greatly informative entry on pantheism. Note Coleridge's objection to pantheism cited therein. Is 'Tintern Abbey' pantheistic? Compare 'Tintern Abbey' in this regard with Emerson's 1836 essay 'Nature.'

2. Compare the way Wordsworth uses Dorothy as a presence in 'Tintern Abbey' with how Coleridge uses his wife, Sara, as a presence in his poem 'The Eolian Harp' ('Effusion XXXV' in *LBRW*).

SECTION FOUR: *LYRICAL BALLADS*, THE SEQUEL

The second edition of *Lyrical Ballads* is a strikingly different work from its predecessor. It is in two volumes and thus is more than twice as long as the first edition. The poems from 1798 appear in a different order in the first volume—with 'Expostulation and Reply' and 'The Tables Turned' opening instead of Coleridge's 'Rime of the Ancyent Marinere.' Disappointed with the sales and reception of the first edition (and believing 'The Ancyent Marinere' was to blame), Wordsworth wanted the second edition to better 'suit the common taste' (*Early Years* 264). The second volume contains mostly new poems written by Wordsworth. Also, Wordsworth wanted to change the title because he did not consider the new poems to be 'lyrical ballads,' but was overruled by his publisher, Thomas Longman, who had just published the poet Mary Robinson's *Lyrical Tales* and who figured that the similarities between titles would only help sales since Robinson was a more established author. The volumes appeared as the work of a single author, 'W. Wordsworth,' although Wordsworth acknowledged the contributions of 'my Friend' in the notes. The second volume opens with 'Hart-Leap Well,' a ballad reminiscent of 'The Thorn' in its hints of the supernatural. It also recalls 'Simon Lee' in its experimentation: the first part of the poem is a seemingly omniscient and action-oriented narrative of an aristocrat's hunting of a deer, but the second part opens with the poet rejecting the tale he has just begun:

> The moving accident is not my trade,
> To curl the blood I have no ready arts;

'Tis my delight, alone in summer shade,
To pipe a simple song to thinking hearts. (97–100)

This stanza goes along with Wordsworth's denunciation of the 'degrading thirst for outrageous stimulation' in the Preface, but it also continues the oxymoronic juxtaposition of *lyric* and *ballad* begun in the first edition by rejecting narrative in favor of a lyric insight that will affect 'thinking hearts.' As in 'Simon Lee,' Wordsworth asks the reader to make meaning by combining thinking with feeling. Although this poem concludes with a more explicit and less political lesson than 'Simon Lee' does, that lesson reveals a deeper faith in the benevolent, almost providential, and morally instructive power of nature. A poem such as 'Hart-Leap Well' in this way supports the traditional critical view that *Lyrical Ballads* shows Wordsworth moving away from politics toward a quasi-pantheistic spirituality or even a secularized Christian perspective. Indeed, many of Wordsworth's new contributions to *Lyrical Ballads* explore the belief he expresses in 'The Old Cumberland Beggar': 'we have all of us one human heart' (146). Even though his friendship with Coleridge remained strong during this time—despite Wordsworth's decision to exclude Coleridge's 'Christabel' and to demote 'The Ancyent Marinere' from lead poem to penultimate one—readers should look for ways in which Wordsworth is doing something different in the 1800 collection and how the 1800 poems differ from the 1798 ones. And readers should consider the ways in which the 1798 poems may be read differently in this new context, and how the new poems may show Wordsworth in increasing command of his powers as a poet.

Poems of Memory, of Innocence and Experience

Since many of the new poems in the 1800 *Lyrical Ballads* were written in Germany, Wordsworth found himself relying on memories of home to supply material for composition. The second poem in volume two is the untitled poem beginning with 'There was a Boy,' which, as Gill notes, Wordsworth originally wrote in the first person as his own remembered experience before adding the final lines about the boy's death (*MW* 731). When Coleridge read the first version, he remarked, 'had I met these lines running wild in the deserts of Arabia, I should have instantly screamed out "Wordsworth!"' (*Letters* 1: 453). Wordsworth later incorporated the poem as part of Book V of *The Prelude*. There, it is one of several 'spots of time.' As a separate work in 1800, it is a wonderfully suggestive poem that shows more than it tells. Moreover, it demonstrates Wordsworth's increasing affinity for blank verse. The first 11 lines comprise the poem's first complete sentence and describe the boy's playing outdoors, culminating in his memorable 'mimic hootings' to the owls. The second sentence (lines 11–16) describes their 'responsive' call, emphasizing the interrelatedness between the child and nature. The first verse-paragraph concludes with the mysterious and ominous implication that the boy hears something more profound in moments of silence that seems to be allegorized by the 'uncertain heaven' reflected in the lake. The final sentence and section of the poem shifts to a shocking juxtaposition of the boy's birthplace and burial-place, then concludes with an emphasis on the 'mute' poet in silent contemplation of the boy's untimely death. This last section of the poem complicates what would have been an auto-biographical fragment by presenting the poet musing upon a version of himself now dead.

Like 'There was a Boy,' 'Nutting' is a blank-verse poem that reflects the poet's inward turn just as he is coming to think about both *The Recluse* and *The Prelude*. Wordsworth identified 'Nutting' as having been intended for the latter, but, unlike 'There was a Boy,' he did not find a place for it in *The Prelude*. From start to finish, the poem explores the dubiousness of memory, beginning mid-line with 'It seems a day,' with subsequent parenthetical equivocation, and ending with the possibility that, in relating the significance of the recalled event, the poet has confused his 'present feelings with the past' (47). On one level, the poem is a fairly realistic portrayal of young boys' destructive playfulness; on another, as a conspicuous footnote in the 1800 volume reveals, it is autobiographical. On a still deeper level, as most critics have recognized, the boy's 'merciless ravage' of the 'virgin scene' has powerful erotic suggestions that might just as probably reflect the behavior of adolescent boys in their nascent sexuality. The natural scene is feminized, and the boy longs to master it. This desire for mastery begins around lines 16 and 17, but its consummation is delayed, giving the description of the act a strangely erotic tension on top of phrases such as those

I have just quoted. Some readers see the action of the poem as a rape or as an oblique treatment of masturbation, replete finally with attendant guilt. The trees 'patiently gave up / Their quiet being' (46–7), and thus cease to live, recalling how Christ 'gave up the ghost' (Mark 15.37; Trott 146). So, when the speaker refers to the 'Spirit' at the end of the poem it has a rich allusiveness that combines with the address to the 'Maiden.' The conclusion of the poem seems to provide a moral lesson about the destruction of nature; but upon closer reading, the 'Spirit' at the end recalls the death, or the giving up of being, of the bower and the allusion to Christ (see Trott). This allusion makes an uneasy connection to the anonymous 'dearest Maiden,' who, referred to as such, recalls the 'virgin scene,' and equates her improbably with the callow young man who destroys the bower. Such behavior seems uncharacteristic of young girls, so we are left wondering what the lesson really is and to whom it is directed. The result is a provocatively ambiguous poem about innocence and experience.

Like William Blake's *Songs of Innocence and of Experience* (1794), many of Wordsworth's poems deal with this theme in seemingly simple and straightforward lyrics. These poems from the 1800 *Lyrical Ballads*—sometimes referred to as 'the Goslar lyrics' because they were written during a miserable winter in Germany—belie their superficial simplicity with darker undercurrents of loss that look forward to more elaborate ruminations in such poems as 'Elegiac Stanzas' and the 'Intimations Ode.' The 1800 edition includes three poems commonly referred to as the 'Matthew poems': 'Lines Written on a Tablet in a School' (later titled 'Matthew'), 'The Two April Mornings,' and 'The Fountain.' In these poems Wordsworth develops a composite character based on his Hawkshead schoolmaster, Reverend William Taylor, and an old storytelling pedlar who would visit the school and who also inspired Armytage in 'The Ruined Cottage.' (This Matthew is not to be confused with the Matthew of 'Expostulation and Reply,' who is based on William Hazlitt; they are altogether different characters.) The Matthew of the Goslar poems is an elderly schoolteacher, nature-lover, father-figure, playmate, and rustic poet; as the dead boy in 'There was a Boy' is a projection of Wordsworth's lost youth, so Matthew is the poet's vision of himself as an old man. The first in the series, beginning 'If Nature, for a favorite Child,' is both elegy and introduction. It describes Matthew's vacillating moods of joy and melancholy, playfulness and contemplation, and provides some insight into the poems that follow. The speaker in the poem reads Matthew's name in a list of former schoolmasters and, troubled by such a slight memorial, provides a general recollection of what the man was like when alive. The poem is rendered more complex by the difficulty the speaker has in bringing the man back to life in verse and by the admitted failure to do so at the end of the poem:

> —Thou soul of God's best earthly mould,
> Thou happy soul, and can it be
> That these two words of glittering gold
> Are all that must remain of thee?

This first Matthew poem is a stark undoing of the long tradition of immortalizing others in verse, or the eternizing conceit, most famously articulated in Shakespeare's sonnet 18 ('Shall I compare thee to a summer's day?'), which concludes, 'So long as men can breathe or eyes can see / So long lives this and this gives life to thee.' 'This' is of course the poem, and it attests to the poet's power more than it does to any particular virtue possessed by the loved one. Concluding as it does with a doubtful rhetorical question, Wordsworth's 'Lines Written on a Tablet in a School' reveals no such confidence, and the two-word gilt inscription thus achieves a permanence even the poem cannot do.

In a way, Matthew does come alive in the succeeding poems, however, as they develop specific recollections, showing Wordsworth's faith in the imaginative work where memory participates. They illustrate Wordsworth's theory of poetic composition—'emotion recollected in tranquillity.' And they demonstrate Matthew doing such through dialogue: both 'The Two April Mornings' and 'The Fountain,' subtitled 'A Conversation,' present the speaker in relation to his past just as the remembered dialogues present his younger self in conversation with the much older man. These are subtle poems about loss and mortality, made even more so by the recognizable distance between the speaker of the poem and the boy who talks with Matthew, even though they are the same person. The boy is surprised by the incongruity of the pleasure of the morning and the melancholy sigh which escapes his companion—although the end of the poem poignantly suggests that the older speaker-poet now has a more profound perspective on the incident. If the April morning—with all of its associations of rebirth—is the site for revelations of mortality and loss, we realize by the end that there are, in a sense, three April mornings: the one that reminds Matthew of his loss, the one Matthew describes, and finally the moment of composition that provides the image of Matthew 'with his bough / Of wilding in his hand' (59–60). But as Matthew's described experience of seeing the lovely living girl has shown, no image or recollection can compensate for the loss of the real loved one. Matthew's image is recalled in abstraction, emphasizing how utterly the corporeal man, like his daughter, no longer exists. Here, memory is not as palliative when it reminds one not of the permanence of nature but rather of the mortality of specific individuals. The symbolism of the 'bough of wilding' is provocative too—the bough having been cut from a living tree.

In 'The Fountain' Wordsworth employs two symbols, the 'spreading oak' and the spring or fountain, to initiate the exchange between the same two characters, suggesting that the former stands for old age and the latter for youth. Here Wordsworth presents the boy and Matthew explicitly as 'friends' despite the age difference. The boy interprets the 'gurgling' of the fountain as a sign of communal play, suggesting that they 'try to match / This water's pleasant tune' with a song of joy (9–10). To the boy the fountain dissolves the difference in age between them, while Matthew understands it differently—it reminds him of his own youth and brings forth tears instead of songs. Matthew's subsequent speech (33–56) is surprisingly dark as he acknowledges wearing a disingenuous 'face of joy': a recognition of decay, alienation from the joy of nature, a consciousness of profound loss, and not so much disappointment as dissatisfaction. It is a grim epiphany that the boy cannot fully appreciate, although he can good-naturedly offer himself as a substitute for Matthew's deceased children. 'Alas,' the old man replies, 'that cannot be' (64). The poem provides no real resolution, only Matthew's obligatory solo performance of the 'witty rhymes' the boy initially had requested they perform together. The song about 'the crazy old church-clock / And the bewildered

chimes' provides a final image of Matthew, a rustic Lear per-
haps, that is uncomfortably linked to madness and death (71–2).
Again, at the close of the poem, memory fails to restore or
rejuvenate. So, readers should consider how Wordsworth puts
memory, imagination, and feeling to different use in these poems
than in, say, 'Tintern Abbey' or 'Daffodils.'

FOR FURTHER STUDY

1. Gill's edition of the *Major Works* provides a series of 'Five
   Elegies' from manuscript that further develop the Matthew
   character but that Wordsworth did not publish as such
   (142–7).
2. Compare one of the Matthew poems with the much-later
   lyrics Theodore Roethke's 'My Papa's Waltz' (1948) or Robert
   Hayden's 'Those Winter Sundays' (1962). Such comparisons
   may provide a sense of how modern Wordsworth's poetry can
   seem.

The Lucy Poems

The Matthew poems, compelling as they are, are not as well-
known as another group of Goslar lyrics that have come to be
known as 'the Lucy poems,' following Matthew Arnold's grouping
of the five poems as a series in his 1879 edition of Wordsworth's
poetry. Wordsworth classified neither the Matthew nor Lucy
poems as such, although it is now commonplace to read each set
as a group: the Lucy poems are 'Strange Fits of Passion Have
I Known,' 'Song' ('She dwelt among th' untrodden ways'),
'A Slumber Did My Spirit Seal,' all three of which were printed
together in the 1800 *Lyrical Ballads*; a fourth, 'Three Years She
Grew in Sun and Shower,' also from 1800 but appearing later in
the volume; and the final one, 'I Travelled among Unknown
Men,' written later and intended to go in the third edition but
published in 1807. More so than most of Wordsworth's other
short lyrics, the Lucy poems are mysterious in and of themselves;
they are made even more so because the poet uncharacteristi-
cally said little about their composition or meaning. Readers
continue to question the identity of Lucy, frequently concluding
that she is meant to represent Dorothy. Coleridge was the first
to suggest such a biographical/allegorical reading with the sug-
gestion that 'Most probably, in some gloomier moment he had

fancied the moment in which his sister might die' (*Letters* 1: 479). Such attempts to read Lucy as Dorothy invariably lead to psychoanalytical interpretations in which Wordsworth fantasizes about his sister's death or sublimates incestuous desires for her or both. Like Matthew, however, Lucy is probably a composite of people Wordsworth knew, and believing her to be a real person is unnecessary for reading the poems.

The three Lucy poems that appear together in the 1800 *Lyrical Ballads*, and which will be the object of our focus, were written in Goslar during the winter of 1798–1799 and perhaps reflect a mood of morbid isolation and depression on the part of the poet. Questions of incest aside, these poems likely have become more popular than the Matthew poems because they are tinged with subtle eroticism and flirt with the age-old titillation in the association between the undeniable physicalities of sex and death. But these poems are peculiar among Wordsworth's poems in this regard and remain endlessly fascinating in their futile attempts to deny those physicalities.

The first to appear in the contents of *Lyrical Ballads* is 'Strange Fits of Passion,' which explores the occasionally morbid psychology of love. The speaker anxiously admits that he has known 'strange fits of passion' and 'dare[s] to tell' of a particular such experience; but he announces he will do so only 'in the lover's ear,' thus fixing the reader ambiguously either as addressee or as voyeur. Is he addressing Lucy, the loved one in the subsequent narrative? Or is he admitting this to a new lover, a role in which the reader is cast? Or is the reader presumably a fellow lover, that is, one who will understand the nature of the experience? Upon first reading, it seems unlikely that it is not Lucy to whom he is confiding, while at the same time the narrative structure, representing her in the third person, suggests otherwise. The narrative part of the poem begins in the second stanza with an odd introduction, 'When she I lov'd, was strong and gay,' suggesting a profound difference between now and then (5). The surprise ending is not so surprising if we are to assume that Lucy is dead. So perhaps the poem is a complex exploration of the guilty 'fond and wayward' thoughts that occasionally go along with love. The speaker confesses that he once considered the shocking possibility that Lucy might be dead when he arrives at her cottage, presumably for a date or assignation; the recollection of this morbid supposition, which may be attached to an excess of passion or perhaps scarcity of passion, is made the more troubling by the eventual actuality of Lucy's death. The bulk of the poem describes the speaker's journey on horseback, during which he becomes transfixed by the moon. The poem's imagery suggests a dream-like state particularly by the optical illusion of the moon's descent as the horse climbs the hill. The speaker claims to have been in a waking sleep, his eye fixed on the moon and dreaming 'sweet dreams' that are 'Kind Nature's gentlest boon!' (17–18). He does not reveal the contents of the dream, however. The trance is made all the more hypnotic by the regularity of the horse's trot; his reverie is broken by the sudden disappearance of the moon, presumably as the horse reaches the top of the hill. The jarring experience of waking from a kind of half-consciousness results in the strange supposition of Lucy's death; but after introducing the poem with a quasi-shameful admission of a unique experience, the speaker finally remarks on it as a universal experience— 'What fond and wayward thoughts will slide / Into a Lover's head' (25–6). 'Fond' here most likely means 'foolish' and 'wayward,' 'capricious'; but what if the two terms are more antithetical? 'Fond' could mean 'affectionate,' while 'wayward' might suggest something darker, more sinister. Is this supposition possibly then related to the contents of the dream? The poem may simply be the shocking awareness of mortality, but this reading does not seem to account for the confessional quality of the opening stanza.

Both the Matthew and the Lucy poems deal with death and the loss of loved one, but the significant difference is that the Lucy poems involve the death of a lover instead of a child. They are love poems in a volume whose love poems are surprisingly ambivalent. In the untitled poem beginning "Tis said, that some have died for love' Wordsworth describes a man whose grief over the death of his lover has driven him mad; the poem closes with the revelation that the speaker fears the happiness of love may not be worth such a severe cost for his beloved or, implicitly, for himself (*MW* 208–10). The Lucy poems, furthermore, expose the solipsistic tendencies of erotic love when the individual lover cannot come to terms with his beloved's otherness or with her individuation. In this way, it is appropriate that 'Lucy' becomes the generic, totemic dead girlfriend of the volume. The 'Song' that follows 'Strange Fits of Passion' is a stark example of this: Lucy is virtually unknowable except as an unknowable entity affixed to specific locations—'th' untrodden ways / Beside the springs of Dove' and finally 'in her Grave' (1–2, 11)—and as an unknowable object of 'praise' who is, if truly isolated from the world, presumably loved only by those 'very few' with familial obligations.

Is the speaker one of the 'very few' to love her? The syntactically ambiguous pronoun 'whom' in line 3 places her in the objective case without answering the question. She continues to be objectified in the most literal sense, represented by grammatically disembodied figurative language in the second stanza, which features first a metaphor and then a simile but contains only an implied subject and verb: *she was* 'A Violet' and *was* 'Fair, as a star' (5–8). I do not mean to imply a misogynistic dehumanization of Lucy as female subject, but I do believe these poems explore an aspect of erotic love that we all know to exist— the difficulty at times of knowing another, even an intimately loved one. What Wordsworth does in a poem such as this is to formalize the problem as poetry in order to recognize its existence. He does this by paradoxically developing the concept of loved one as cipher. The final stanza brilliantly and ambiguously asserts this:

> She *liv'd* unknown, and few could know
>   When Lucy ceas'd to be;
> But she is in her Grave, and Oh!
>   The difference to me. (9–12)

The poem ends with a final mystery regarding the speaker's relationship to the dead girl. Does he know her only in her death? The exclamation 'Oh!' literally is a cipher—a zero—that rhymes with 'know,' an inarticulate expression that says nothing but presumably everything about the speaker's feelings for Lucy. What is the 'difference'? The difference between Lucy alive and Lucy dead? This the poem has resisted showing us by giving us only static—and permanent—natural imagery, thus making a profound point about an unutterable grief and an unknowable lover/other. These poems thus reveal a darker side to Wordsworth's poetic faith demonstrated in 'Tintern Abbey' and throughout *The Prelude*, for here imagination, narrative, poetry itself seem insufficient for negotiating alterity, or otherness. Lucy herself cannot be imagined.

The idea of death and permanence is most provocatively explored in the shortest lyric of the five Lucy poems, 'A Slumber Did My Spirit Seal.' It may be the most commented-upon eight lines in all of English literature, beginning with Coleridge's proclamation of it as a 'sublime Epitaph' (*Letters* 1: 479). Such a claim is potentially oxymoronic since the sublime suggests greatness or magnitude, while an epitaph usually is short enough to fit on a headstone. But as the diversity and depth of interpretation shows, the poem is sublime in that its dimensions may be impossible to measure. My reading of the poem follows from the issues discussed above, although I will resist fixing a determinate interpretation on it. The greatness of the poem is its inscrutability, although its apparent symmetry invites reading it formally in terms of oppositions. The absence of a title and the shortness of the poem on the page visually suggest a totality that clearly divides itself into the two stanzas that comprise the poem. And with a poem of only 48 words, the reader should expect to parse and to interpret with precision, assuming that the poet has selected each word with great care.

What sorts of oppositions are suggested even in the first line? Obviously, we see 'slumber' in contrast to waking, to 'seal' contrasting with 'to open.' But even 'a slumber' versus 'many slumbers' already implies what is evident soon enough—that the slumber is death. He calls it a 'slumber' because he is still coming to terms with the reality of death. Curiously, though, the word 'spirit' is not associated with the deceased but with the speaker— 'my spirit.' This death has closed up his 'spirit'—but how? By ending his happiness? By closing him off from others now that he has lost his loved one? Or does it mean to seal as in to stamp or to make an impression upon something? This 'slumber' has marked his 'spirit'? It is the closest the poem comes to articulating the speaker's feelings in response to the death, and clearly this slumber has marked a change that contradicts his previous condition: 'I had no human fears' (2). How does this previous state of having no 'human fears' differ from having his 'spirit' sealed? Both lines suggest a kind of spiritual limitation, except that his previous state failed to account for the human condition of mortality. The colon that ends the second line is well-placed, for it explains how wrong he was: 'She seem'd a thing that could not feel / The touch of earthly years' (3–4). Clearly, this slumber has exposed his naivety and the profound limitations of his desire for her to stay the same, to remain fixed in a condition that obviates 'human fears.' Heather Glen describes these lines as 'the libidinous inability to recognize the separateness of that which is desired' (287). The all-consuming erotic desire for the loved object has failed to acknowledge her humanity, and this recognition, as much as the loss itself, results in a profound marking or delimiting of the speaker's 'spirit.'

Controversies regarding the interpretation of this poem generally arise from the question of whether or not the second stanza concludes the poem with consolation or not. Decades ago, F. W. Bateson argued that the poem ends in a celebration of the unity of nature, whereas Cleanth Brooks saw in its conclusion a despairing image of cold inhuman nature. In the final stanza, the speaker does seem to accept the reality of Lucy's death but does so in language that is either starkly obvious or bitterly ironic: 'No motion has she now, no force; / She neither hears nor sees' (5–7). These lines are ironic because they seem to be the literal realization of what previously had precluded his 'human fears'—that Lucy herself was not human, not mortal, and thus not alive. In contrast to the first stanza, this one provides no significant commentary on the speaker's emotional attachment to Lucy. Whereas in 'Strange Fits of Passion' the speaker compares Lucy to 'a rose in June' and in 'She Dwelt Among th' Untrodden Ways' he uses natural imagery to remember her as she was when alive, what is most striking about 'A Slumber Did My Spirit Seal' is how the poet concludes by describing her without obviously figurative language and by imagining her as she is now, dead in her grave: 'Roll'd round in earth's diurnal course / With rocks and stones and trees!' (7–8). In a way, the poem concludes with the image of Lucy's becoming one again with nature—from dust to dust, as in Genesis 3. 19. Although this is a natural consolation, we are reminded of the speaker's impression of Lucy in line 3 as 'a thing' while alive and may find it somewhat disturbing that the poem ends with his delusion of her inhumanity confirmed. Again, the living Lucy is an unknowable impossibility. Has she achieved immortality as part of the dynamic generative cycle of life—'earth's diurnal course'—or merely achieved the static condition—'a thing that could not feel'—imposed upon her while she was alive? The reader may opt for a more sentimental reading, but these three poems also interrogate the extent to which lovers can truthfully know one another and whether desire can transcend the self. Love is forever mired in subjectivity. The Lucy poems are dark reminders of the psychological—even ontological—isolation a lover may feel, even when intimately connected to another person. And with the Matthew poems, the Lucy poems show Wordsworth struggling with issues of subjective experience that are positive in relation to nature but become more complicated when other people are involved. They are ahead of their time.

FOR FURTHER STUDY

1. The ballad 'Ruth' is another poem from 1800 that explores the dangers of love; study the poem in terms of what Susan J. Wolfson refers to as the 'heroine's enchantment by narrative' (72).

The Pastoral Poems: 'The Brothers' and 'Michael'

The new ballads in the 1800 *Lyrical Ballads*, such as 'Hart-Leap Well,' 'Ellen Irwin,' 'The Two Thieves,' and 'Ruth,' are more straightforward narrative poems. Other narrative poems that are similar to ballads receive from Wordsworth the qualified subtitle 'A Pastoral'—'The Oak and the Broom,' 'The Idle Shepherd Boys,' and 'The Pet Lamb.' The 1800 *Lyrical Ballads* as well as the subsequent 1802 and 1805 editions all end with the narrative poem 'Michael, A Pastoral Poem,' and the 1800 table of contents also identifies 'The Brothers' as 'A Pastoral Poem.' These are narratives about working-class country people, but Wordsworth's designation of them as *pastoral* has something of a subversive quality given the classical tradition of pastoral poetry and its conventions, which involve the extreme idealization of rural life in poems populated by amorous shepherds and nymphs. The pastoral was revived in late sixteenth-century English literature by Spenser, Sidney, and Marlowe, and it continued throughout the seventeenth and eighteenth centuries, notably practiced by Milton in his pastoral elegy, 'Lycidas.'

However, by the time Oliver Goldsmith's poem *The Deserted Village* appeared in 1770 to celebrate the simple joys of eighteenth-century country living, other poets had become frustrated with what they considered unrealistic portrayals of the rural poor. In 1783, George Crabbe published *The Village* as a poetic rejoinder to Goldsmith's idealizations with the explicit intention to show 'What forms a real picture of the poor' (*LBRW* 275). Following Crabbe, Robert Southey's pastorals of the 1790s employ Virgil's designation *Eclogues* to articulate radical political views and humanitarian concerns regarding the poor and disenfranchised—such as Botany Bay convicts transported to Australia.

In a similar way, Wordsworth's 'The Brothers' and 'Michael' are ironic 'pastorals' because they subvert the idealized tradition and replace the stock nymphs and swains with more realistic portraits of rural life. Like Southey, Wordsworth wrote them with an eye to politics and even sent the book to liberal states-man Charles James Fox, noting that 'The Brothers' and 'Michael' were 'written with a view to shew that men who do not wear fine cloaths can feel deeply' (*Early Years* 315). (When Fox replied to Wordsworth, he remarked that he did not feel blank verse to be appropriate 'for subjects which are to be treated of with sim-plicity' [quoted in Woof 106].) These poems are set in the rural Lake District, where industrialization and commercialization appeared to Wordsworth to be causing the disappearance of small proprietors of inherited land. Wordsworth's concern for the plight of rural people in the north of England was heightened by his decision to return to the Lake District and to set up residence with Dorothy in Grasmere upon returning from Germany. These two poems were written during the first year in the valley that would be Wordsworth's home for the rest of his life.

'The Brothers' and 'Michael' also are examples of how, as he explains in the Preface, the feeling developed in a narrative poem is more important than the plot, which in both of these poems is a bit more elaborate than in some of the 1798 ballads. For both poems Wordsworth eschews the ballad form in favor of blank verse. 'The Brothers' is an ostensibly dramatic poem, as the dialogue between the two characters appears on the page almost like a script. Leonard Ewbank, a sailor who has returned home to resume his former life as a shepherd, converses with the village Priest, who does not recognize him. The deeper drama of the poem unfolds as Leonard asks innocuous questions about the village and its inhabitants; in response the Priest gradually relays details of Leonard's own checkered life and that of his brother, James, including James' death by sleepwalking off of a cliff. (The death-by-sleepwalking element is based on a true story that Wordsworth and Coleridge heard from an old woman while walking through the region.) As the poem continues, the Priest does most of the talking, as Leonard becomes increasingly taciturn, but the literally dramatic scenario causes the reader to surmise Leonard's emotional response to the story of his brother's shocking demise. Leonard departs without revealing his identity, only to do so later in a letter to the Priest—before returning to sea, his last tie to the village now broken. It is a stark and powerful poem that operates on a level beyond plot. But other important features are worth noting too: the indirect manner by which Leonard attempts to learn information from the Priest, the Priest's opening remarks about tourists to the region, and James's extraordinary death and how it is unconsciously connected to James's longing for his lost brother, who, again, is the one listening to the story. Moreover, the way the Priest ends his tale and how the poem ends may be compared to the conclusion of 'The Ruined Cottage.'

As the letter to Fox indicates, Wordsworth understood that the growing crisis of rural life was the necessity behind the decision of families such as the Ewbanks to disperse, one or more members having to leave the country for greater opportunities. Like Walter Ewbank, Michael, the shepherd in our second poem here, is one of those men 'who daily labour on their own little properties,' land which they have inherited, and who are 'rapidly disappearing' as their sons are forced to seek livings elsewhere (*Early Years* 314). Wordsworth sees this economic exigency as a threat to 'domestic affections,' familial bonds, and to the independence, prosperity, and health of rural societies (*Early Years* 314–15). New economic circumstances bring with them new threats: Michael, because of a nephew's default on a debt for which the shepherd is now responsible, will lose his land. 'If these fields of ours,' he says to his wife, Isabel, 'Should pass into a Stranger's hand, I think / That I could not lie quiet in my grave' (240–2). Michael's dilemma, as he sees it, is that he must either sell some of his land or send his son, Luke, to the city to earn money.

He fails to see any other opportunity at home. As Michael himself says, 'Where every one is poor / What can be gained?' (264–5). 'The Brothers' and 'Michael' are ironic pastorals, indeed. In the character of Michael, moreover, Wordsworth, as he wrote in a letter, wanted to show 'two of the most powerful affections of the human heart'—family and inherited property (*Early Years* 322).

Like the opening of the 'Lines Left upon a Seat in a Yew-Tree,' 'Michael' begins with a direct address to the reader declaring that the pleasure of the setting is likely to be missed. The poem begins and ends at the same spot. Similarly, the speaker, a poet, possibly Wordsworth himself, advises that appreciation of the poem will require what he has learned already from Nature, the ability 'to feel / For passions that were not my own' and to read 'the heart of man and human life' (30–1, 33). Moreover, like 'Hart-Leap Well,' 'Michael' centers around a seemingly insignificant spot that presents a story—'a struggling heap of unhewn stones' (17). These rocks, the unfinished sheep-fold, become a symbol of the broken 'covenant' between Michael and his son Luke (424). The notion of covenant is important as 'Michael' carries a richer biblical allusiveness than is common in Wordsworth's poetry of this period. Obviously, the parable of the Prodigal Son from, appropriately enough, the Gospel of Luke, chapter 15, is an ironic intertext. Similarly, Michael as a father may be compared (favorably or unfavorably) with Abraham in Genesis. The poem, furthermore, is full of more obvious symbols than we find in much of Wordsworth's poetry: the light by which the family's cottage is known, 'the Evening Star,' is a 'public Symbol' of their work ethic (146, 137); the 'clipping tree' is a symbol of daily labour and interrelation between human and animal as well as a site of paternal discipline, 'fond correction and reproof' (179, 183); and the staff Michael makes for Luke even has an epic iconicity, complete with a history like Odysseus's bow or Achilles' shield (190–203).

Overall, Michael's property stands as a symbol and memorial for the continuity of family: as Wordsworth wrote to Fox, 'Their little tract of land serves as a kind of permanent rallying point for their domestic feelings, as a tablet upon which they are written which makes them objects of memory in a thousand instances when they would otherwise be forgotten' (*Early Years* 314–15). Already an old man when he becomes a father, Michael has a powerful connection with the land, even its animals, with the fields and hills that are 'his living Being, even more / Than his own Blood'; these have 'laid / Strong hold on his affections' and are 'A pleasurable feeling of blind love, / The pleasure which there is in life itself' (75–9). Against the powerful symbolism of the land is the anonymity and transience of 'the dissolute city' where a young man may give 'himself to evil courses' and disappear in 'ignominy and shame'—which is what happens to Luke (453–4). (As Book VII of *The Prelude* shows, Wordsworth was no lover of the city.) Compared with his father, Luke is too young to feel this connection to the earth, and the hold the land lays on his affections is not strong enough to bring him home. The penultimate verse paragraph, beginning 'There is a comfort in the strength of love,' has been called one of the finest passages in Wordsworth's poetry, particularly as it includes the poignant detail that 'many and many a day' Michael went to the spot where he and Luke were to build the sheep-fold but 'never lifted up a single stone' (457–81). As this is a poem that students today frequently find to be boring, we might consider how subtle, restrained, and unsentimental a poem it is—the most sensational aspect of the story, Luke's dissolution, is told in five lines. Dorothy Wordsworth's *Grasmere Journal*, moreover, reveals that the actual decrepit sheep-fold that inspired 'Michael' was 'built nearly in the form of a heart' (26). Wordsworth, therefore, obviously rejected what surely would have a potently sentimental emblem for the poem. Finally, Wordsworth presents Michael either as having been made noble through his grief and disappointment or as having been utterly defeated by it.

FOR FURTHER STUDY

1. Is Michael selfish? Does he lay too heavy a burden on Luke?
2. Wordsworth replaced Coleridge's unfinished 'Christabel' with his own 'Michael' as the concluding poem of the 1800 *Lyrical Ballads*. How might the inclusion of 'Christabel' have affected the way we read the other poems? How might we read the two poems in relation to one another, as potential companion poems? Similarly, since 'Tintern Abbey' closes the first volume in 1800 and 'Michael' the second, how might these poems go together?

3. 'The Old Cumberland Beggar' is a more overtly political poem than 'Michael' is and was written two years earlier; can you discern a shift in Wordsworth's politics that might account for a seemingly more muted approach in 'Michael'?

4. Consider *Home at Grasmere* both as part of the larger epic project *The Recluse* and as a more positive use of the pastoral tradition: how does Wordsworth reconcile pastoral and epic in this long (and charming) poem?

SECTION FIVE: *POEMS, IN TWO VOLUMES*

Wordsworth finished the first complete draft of *The Prelude* in 1805; it did not appear in print, however, until 1850 (see Chapters 2 and 4). Wordsworth's blank-verse masterpiece and a significant portion of *The Recluse*, *Home at Grasmere*, also in blank verse, are framed by songwriting. And while the editions of *Lyrical Ballads* contain such superlative achievements in blank verse as 'Tintern Abbey,' 'The Old Cumberland Beggar,' and 'Michael,' every poem in Wordsworth's 1807 *Poems, in Two Volumes* rhymes. After completing the 1799 *Two-Part Prelude* and a possibly complete draft of *Home at Grasmere* in 1800 and before recommencing work on the poem in 1804, Wordsworth wrote almost exclusively in the lyric mode. Obviously, the second edition of *Lyrical Ballads* contained many lyric poems; after its publication in 1800, however, Wordsworth for a time wrote few poems until the late winter and spring of 1802, when he became interested in lyric forms again. As Jared Curtis has established, the poems from early 1802 provide the impetus for the 1807 volume and came into being almost miraculously, given the emotional and financial pressures he endured.

Indeed, 1802 is a momentous year for Wordsworth. He published the famous expanded Preface to *Lyrical Ballads*, he continued to feel economic distress resulting from the ongoing financial dispute between the Wordsworth family and Lord Lonsdale's estate, and he was able to visit his daughter Caroline in France and establish an agreement with her mother, Annette Vallon, before marrying Mary Hutchinson in October. From this time until 1805, his efforts in blank verse were focused on *The Prelude*; but averse to publishing this work until either completion of *The Recluse* or his own death, Wordsworth felt that, after seven years, he needed to publish something new. Writing to Walter Scott in November 1806, Wordsworth announced that he reluctantly would send to press two volumes 'entirely of small pieces' and admits that 'the day when my long work will be finished seems farther and farther off.' Still, he expresses some pride in the new collection and the 'hope that it will one day or other be thought well of by the Public' (*Middle Years* 1: 96). Despite some ambivalence toward *Poems, in Two Volumes*, Wordsworth does reveal the courage of the convictions expressed in the 1805 *Prelude*, so one valuable way to read these poems is to do so in light of that work. For instance, Wordsworth writes to his friend Lady Beaumont that he does not fear 'censure,' understanding that to many 'respectable persons' these poems may appear 'insignificant'—not to mention the opinion of 'London wits and witlings.' He expresses hope that the poems will appeal to 'grave, kindly-natured, worthy persons' yet feels, especially after having written *The Prelude*, that 'their imagination has slept; and the voice which is the voice of my Poetry without Imagination cannot be heard' (*Middle Years* 1: 146).

While he was somewhat uncertain about lyric poetry, Wordsworth's publication of *Poems, in Two Volumes* marks a new phase in his career, particularly as it is the first volume of poems not specifically associated with *Lyrical Ballads*. The book is, in a sense, his first major solo performance—although he is identified on the title page as 'Author of the Lyrical Ballads.' Wordsworth is crafting and solidifying his public persona; and while *The Prelude* is indispensable ultimately in reading Wordsworth's poetry, I want to remind the reader that the poems in this final volume of the 'great decade' presume an audience that Wordsworth actually wants to reach—an audience that is not just Coleridge. Thus this volume is largely free of Coleridge's influence, and so reading *Poems, in Two Volumes* will bring this chapter full circle, taking us back to the first publication of the 'Daffodils.'

While poems such as 'The Sailor's Mother,' 'Beggars,' 'Alice Fell,' and 'The Blind Highland Boy' are ostensibly in the vein of *Lyrical Ballads*, the majority of the collection has a freshness of lyrical expression, simple language, formal experimentation, and intense subjectivity—qualities to which many contemporary critics and readers objected. It is really *Poems, in Two Volumes*—not *Lyrical Ballads*—that caused the greater uproar, at least until the publication of *The Excursion* in 1814 (see Chapter 4). And, I suspect, the abundance of poems about flowers, birds, and butterflies might make the book a challenge for some readers today. But we should not discount the simpler, sometimes playful poems that have charms and powers of their own—see, for instance, 'Alice Fell,' 'Fidelity,' 'The Kitten and the Falling Leaves,' 'To the Cuckoo,' or 'To the Spade of a Friend.' Upon closer inspection, even the simplest poems might prove rewarding. 'To the Cuckoo,' for instance, undoubtedly inspired Shelley's more-famous poem 'To a Sky-lark' and Keats's masterful 'Ode to a Nightingale.' All three poems explore the imaginative implications of hearing the song of a seemingly invisible bird. As Wordsworth points out in the 1815 Preface to his collected poems, 'To the Cuckoo' is an important instance of 'the Imagination acting upon an individual image' (*MW* 632). Wordsworth's choice of epigraph, however, does belie the darker complexity of some of these lyrics. The title pages of both volumes give the following lines from Virgil as an apology for their light cheerfulness: '*Posterius graviore sono tibi Musa loquetur / Nostra: dabunt cum securos mihi tempora fructus.*' One contemporary reviewer translates the epigraph as 'Hereafter, at better opportunity, our muse shall speak to you in a more impressive tone' (Woof 178). Undoubtedly it is an oblique reference to the hoped-for publication of *The Recluse* and an homage and concession to Coleridge: Coleridge's departure to Malta no doubt enabled Wordsworth to nurse the lyric vice, while also working on *The Prelude*. (One lyric, 'A Complaint,' does address Coleridge's absence without identifying him.)

People in the 1807 Poems

The Coleridge with the most emphatic presence in *Poems, in Two Volumes* is not S. T. but his son Hartley. Wordsworth's 'To H. C., Six Years Old' presents a particular challenge because we know too much about Hartley's family and his ultimate fate: he inherited his father's addictive personality and suffered from alcoholism, dying in 1849, the year before the death of Wordsworth, who attended the funeral. It is difficult, therefore, to avoid these facts when reading the poem, which then becomes considerably more poignant and seemingly prophetic. Even so, Hartley is Wordsworth's inspiration for the 'best philosopher' of the 'Intimations Ode' (see below), and the poem has some rather jarring modulations of tone that make for complicated interpretation—it is part playful and part doomful—and possibly for ironic reading against the Ode. In the 'Intimations Ode,' the child is closer to God and the adult an alien of Heaven; here, the child is celebrated in his strangeness but this gives rise to 'many fears' for his future years (13). Hartley is presented in his childhood as heavenly and immortal, a symbol of the imagination; paradoxically, however, the speaker so profoundly cannot imagine the child as becoming a functioning adult that he predicts either death or the impossibility of perpetual innocence. It is an ambivalent poem that, unlike the Lucy poems, does imagine the child's separateness and actuality but that also poignantly fails to imagine a future for him that is not fixed in the poem's brand of poetic immortality. Interestingly, 'To H. C., Six Years Old' later would end up in Wordsworth's classification of poems 'Referring to the Period of Childhood,' along with the much less ambiguous 'We Are Seven' and 'Anecdote for Fathers.' The poem, moreover, found an admirer in Blake, who could be a severe critic of Wordsworth's poetry.

Predictably Dorothy Wordsworth is a presence in a number of the poems. She appears, oddly enough, as 'Lucy' in the untitled poem beginning 'Among all lovely things my Love had been' and as 'Emmeline' in 'The Sparrow's Nest.' The former traditionally is not considered to be one of the Lucy poems because it is based on an actual experience brother and sister had in 1795 and was written down in 1802—two years after the Goslar poems were written—and because two earlier drafts of the poem had 'Emma' and 'Mary' for 'Lucy.' It also has some biographical complexity, as Wordsworth presented the finished draft as a memento to Dorothy who immediately sent it to her brother's fiancée, Mary Hutchinson (as well as to Coleridge on the same day). Biography aside, Wordsworth's decision to use the name again in this poem is worth noting, although, unlike the Lucy poems, the poet dropped it from his collected works after 1807. Both poems record with potentially symbolic artifacts—a glowworm and a sparrow's egg—memorable experiences he and his sister enjoyed.

'The Sparrow's Nest' is a more complicated poem of memory, seemingly beginning with an address to the reader in the present tense—'Look, five blue eggs are gleaming there!' When the poem shifts into the past tense, the opening then appears to be a kind of invocation to his own memory. The eggs in the maternal nest form an interesting contrast with the setting, 'hard by / My Father's House' (7–8); his younger sister's ambivalence toward the nest provokes the speaker's more expansive experience and appreciation of Nature and of human emotion.

Poems, in Two Volumes reflect the interests and concerns of an older man, particularly a now-married man. Not known for amorous verse, Wordsworth presents here a love poem—albeit an unconventional one—for his wife, Mary. Like Shakespeare's sonnet 120, 'My Mistress' eyes are nothing like the sun,' 'She Was a Phantom of Delight' is a tribute to a real woman as opposed to an unattainable ideal. The poem pays its homage by gradually undoing the lover's inclination to idealize his beloved. The first stanza, which reads at first like flattering hyperbole, shows how such portrayals are inhumanly reductive and fundamentally egocentric: she is 'A lovely Apparition sent / To be a moment's ornament' and 'A dancing Shape, an Image gay, / To haunt, to startle, and way-lay' (3–4, 9–10). The emphasis is upon what she does for the lover, without much regard for her own personhood. In the second stanza, Wordsworth charts a progression in the speaker's/lover's recognition of her as 'A Spirit, yet a Woman too!' (12). He begins, 'upon nearer view,' to appreciate her in the quotidian rounds of ordinary life (11). Although one might be startled by his description of her, 'A Creature not too bright or good / For human nature's daily food,' he, again like Shakespeare, would rather love a real woman instead of an angel because she is able to provide him with, not the stuff of dreams, but with the 'food' of mortal existence. In this way, the poem looks toward Elizabeth Barrett Browning's *Sonnets from the Portuguese* and its emphasis on the need for mortal sustenance. The third stanza of the poem brings us to the present: 'And now I see with eye serene / The very pulse of the machine' (21–2). Wordsworth means to complicate our response to the poem with such a line, ironically emphasizing the mechanics of the organism in order to force a recognition of her full corporeality. When he comes to praise her as 'A perfect Woman' (27), we understand that this statement is no longer hyperbole: she is not an impossible ideal but is, rather, 'perfect' in that she is complete in and of herself, lacking nothing that is essential for the speaker's admiration. She has the powers requisite of a friend, wife, and mother—and yet a spark remains, 'something of an angel light,' but it is not enough to outshine her mortal attributes (30).

The 1807 collection is replete with actual people, contrasting strikingly with the composite figures and fictional personages of the 1798 and 1800 *Lyrical Ballads*. This is a clear turning point in the poet's work. And while many of these same types continue to appear, Wordsworth's foregrounding of eminent names in the poems certainly would affect the publicity of the volume and its reception, as well as the construction of his public persona. The series of 'Miscellaneous Sonnets,' which includes his excellent sonnets 'Composed upon Westminster Bridge' and 'The World Is Too Much with Us,' closes with an homage to his friend and benefactor, the long-deceased Raisley Calvert. Figures from history such as Rob Roy and Michelangelo appear in stark contrast to one another and in very different formal contexts: 'Rob Roy's Grave' begins the second volume as part of a series 'Poems Written During a Tour of Scotland'; it has a rustic tavern-song-like quality, and opens with a comparison between Roy and Robin Hood, playing on an affinity between England and Scotland and implicitly celebrating the centenary of union between the two countries. The poem thus perhaps makes an oblique commentary on the 1800 union between Great Britain and Ireland. The three Michelangelo sonnets highlight Wordsworth's poetic mastery by performing the difficult feat of translating both the Italian form and the Italian language; moreover, the sonnets he chose to translate are exemplary of the Renaissance artist's piety and strike notes that seem profoundly un-Wordsworthian if one thinks of the poet only as a Nature-worshipper.

In addition to creating characters, *Poems, in Two Volumes* shows Wordsworth developing themes based upon well-known people and thus also upon the reader's knowledge of them. This includes several of Wordsworth's contemporaries and attendant references to current events—chiefly the ongoing Napoleonic Wars. 'The Character of the Happy Warrior,' Wordsworth's footnote informs us, is a tribute to Admiral Horatio Nelson, who died victorious at the Battle of Trafalgar. The sonnets are also

steeped in the politics of the Napoleonic Wars and related con-
flicts. Napoleon himself is considered and rejected in the sonnet
'I grieved for Buonaparte,' which initiated Wordsworth's serious
practice in the form after Milton's example (see Chapter 2). The
discipline of the form and the rigor of Michelangelo's piety in
the translated sonnets establish a pattern of austere virtue that
reemerges in Wordsworth's more overtly political sonnets. Fol-
lowing 'Miscellaneous Sonnets,' the series 'Sonnets Dedicated to
Liberty' begins with three patriotic sonnets written in France and
directly precedes the Napoleon sonnet. The series also includes
a sonnet to Gustav IV, King of Sweden, who at a time of great
hardship maintained a strong alliance with Britain against
Napoleon. More famous today is 'To Toussaint L'Ourverture,' a
remarkable sonnet praising the former Governor of Haiti who
resisted Napoleon and who had recently died in a Paris prison.
Wordsworth wishes to conjure Milton's spirit in 'London, 1802,'
which is followed by 'Great Men have been among us' celebrat-
ing other seventeenth-century heroes from the English Civil Wars
who fought against the Royalists for the Republican cause.
Stylistically as well as thematically, the political sonnets sit in
uneasy yet provocative relations with the simpler-seeming lyrics
of the 1807 collection. Along with these sonnets on piety and
virtue, the anomalous 'Ode to Duty' reveals an ascetic strain in
Wordsworth that explains his personal admiration for Milton
but that seems to contrast sharply with the abundance of joy
elsewhere in *Poems, in Two Volumes*. In some ways he is crafting
an image of himself not as a 'Romantic' but as a new Puritan.
These poems, with their political and social engagements, image
Wordsworth standing among those he admires as a public fig-
ure—not wandering lonely as a cloud.

FOR FURTHER STUDY

1. A particularly noteworthy presence in *Poems, in Two Volumes*
   is that of Wordsworth's French daughter, Caroline, to whom
   Wordsworth refers in the famous sonnet beginning 'It is a
   beauteous Evening, calm and free.' During a brief peace, fol-
   lowing the Treaty of Amiens, Wordsworth was able to revisit
   France and see his nine-year-old daughter for the first time;
   he and the child's mother, Annette Vallon, were able to agree
   upon an arrangement for parental support, thus enabling

Wordsworth in good conscience to marry Mary Hutchinson. How necessary is it to know this information? Interestingly, some readers, without it, assume the girl is Dorothy. Does knowing the girl is his daughter have any effect upon interpreting the sonnet's theme and its potential relationship with the 'Intimations Ode' (see below)?

2. The profundity of 'The Solitary Reaper' among so many poems about the songs of birds is the greater mystery in the girl's song. Compare the speaker's response to the song he does not understand to other poems that explore his responses to non-human Nature. What is the speaker able to intuit about the subject of the song without understanding its language? What is the poem saying, then, about the ability to intuit meaning when communication seems impossible? Is this memorable experience any different from that with the daffodils?

3. In the sonnet 'The world is too much with us,' in what ways are 'we' 'out of tune' and with what? Why would the speaker 'rather be / A Pagan suckled in a creed outworn'?

4. How does Wordsworth's exquisite sonnet 'Composed upon Westminster Bridge' while describing the city, an atypical subject for him, manage to be quintessentially Wordsworthian? See Dorothy Wordsworth's brief account of crossing Westminster Bridge (123).

The Leech-Gatherer

Along with the forest girl in 'We Are Seven' and Martha Ray in 'The Thorn,' the Leech-Gatherer from 'Resolution and Independence' stands chief among the most iconic figures in Wordsworth's poetry, nearly rivaling Coleridge's Ancient Mariner. He too is based on a real person and on an actual encounter Wordsworth and his sister had in 1800. Dorothy Wordsworth's journal records they had met a beggar who formerly had been a Leech-Gatherer but who had been driven to poverty by the scarcity of leeches (23–4). Wordsworth obviously could not resist the poetic potential of the old man's former occupation and presents the man in his poem as still active in the business in order to stress the 'independence' signified by the title. The Leech-Gatherer is an emblem of fortitude and endurance. The 'resolution' in the poem is the poet's determination to persist in his own efforts—especially when, as he learns from the Leech-Gatherer, others less fortunate remain undeterred by adversities greater than being an unsuccessful poet who cannot complete (or even begin) *The Recluse*. The Leech-Gatherer is the poet's doppelganger; so, unlike a poem such as 'Simon Lee' that urges its readers to think, 'Resolution and Independence' turns that exhortation back upon the poet, who actually is the subject of the poem. According to biographer Mary Moorman, it is 'the poem in which we see more of Wordsworth than any other poem' (538).

If so, Wordsworth presents himself with as much ambivalence as he does any other character. In 'Resolution and Independence' the poet is frustrated with the limitations of Romantic subjectivity, a position which Wordsworth seems to wholeheartedly embrace. The first two stanzas find Wordsworth modulating perspective via tense: these stanzas establish an immediacy that the third stanza retracts with an emphatic recapitulation of the opening imagery, this time in the past tense: 'I was . . .,' 'I saw . . .,' 'I heard . . .' (15–17). This oscillation is jarring, but we see that it corresponds with the speaker's fluctuating mood: 'As high as we have mounted in delight / In our dejection do we sink as low' (24–5). This important observation, which rings true regarding the creative temperament, is framed by another shift to a disoriented present that seems to speak for the poet in the act of composition as much as it does the recollected impression of that morning (29–42). The poet is troubled by what we call today 'free-floating anxiety': just as he admits himself 'a happy Child of earth,' he must confront vague 'fears, and fancies' about the future (31, 27). The poems that conclude this chapter—this one, 'Elegiac Stanzas,' and the 'Intimations Ode'—each in their own way challenge the 'cheerful faith' expressed earlier in 'Tintern Abbey.' Here he doubts the 'pleasant thought' he has always held, 'As if life's business were a summer mood,' that 'all needful things would come unsought' (36–8). He knows now he has to work for it, but with that acknowledgment comes the crippling possibility of failure.

The poem is very much about the rise and fall of spirit characteristic of poets and artists; as Anthony Conran long ago pointed out, as such, the poem is not without comic touches. Indeed, the poem may be read surprisingly as having a certain degree of self-parody, mocking those very characteristics of the brooding genius that delineate the Romantic caricature. As he becomes absorbed in self-pitying comparisons of himself with the suicidal poet Chatterton and the indigent poet Burns, he poignantly but aptly observes that creative types do have a tendency to 'deify' themselves, and thus create for themselves a kind of solipsistic joy that may collapse in the face of reality and the painful deflation of all ego and ambition—this way leads to 'despondency and madness' (49). At this point the Leech-Gatherer appears, metaphorically interposing himself between Wordsworth and the dead poets who trouble his thoughts. If this is a poem about the poet being a poet, the couplet 'I saw a Man before me unawares: / The oldest Man he seemed that ever wore grey hairs' appears to be comically, self-referentially weak (55–6). More impressive perhaps are the elaborate similes in lines 64–70—much has been made of them by commentators, including Wordsworth himself in his 1815 Preface (see *MW* 633). Wordsworth's comments here are primarily about the conjunctive rendering of disparate imagery by the imagination and not about lines in context. But as a converse answer to the couplet above, the stanza seems comically overblown. For example, the simile comparing the old man to the 'huge Stone' is distended by comparing that stone to a 'Sea-beast'; it is a double figure, a simile within a simile. While this is wildly inventive, in context, the stanza sticks out as Poetry, with a capital *P*, as a particularly self-conscious imaginative exertion of figurative language on the part of the poet that appears nowhere else in the poem. The poem continues with the poet engaging this almost-otherworldly figure in mundane small talk and becomes so lost in reverie that he ignores the old man's answers to his insipid questions. As we read the poem, we should keep in mind that the poet himself concludes it practically laughing at himself in 'scorn.' The poem is, after all, about 'the Leech-gatherer on the lonely moor'—a possibly ridiculous subject (as contemporary reviewers confirmed) that belies the gravitas of the similes in 64–70. At the end of the poem he chides himself for being so wishy-washy about his vocation and implicitly resolves to become the poet-teacher of *The Excursion* and beyond. The irony of our focus in this chapter on 'the great decade' is that, by the end of it, as this poem shows, Wordsworth seems ready to leave that version of himself behind to become the poet he wanted to be. But that poet is one whom today's readers do not appreciate nearly as much.

FOR FURTHER STUDY

1. Lest my commentary above give the impression that 'Resolution and Independence' is wholly comic, I should point out that it has a complex textual history and an intricate intertextual relationship with Coleridge's grim masterpiece 'Dejection: An Ode' as well as with the 'Intimations Ode.' Jared Curtis and Lucy Newlyn have provided important commentary on the poem and its original draft, titled 'The Leech-Gatherer,' studying the evolution of its theme. See particularly Gene W. Ruoff's study of the two drafts in relation to the two odes by Coleridge and Wordsworth. Still, even in this more sober light, 'Resolution and Independence,' you may find, emerges as oddly affirmative in its ludicrousness.

'A Deep Distress Hath Humanized My Soul': 'Elegiac Stanzas'

The benediction that closes 'Tintern Abbey' comes with the assurance that 'Nature never did betray / The heart that loved her' (123–4). The penultimate work in the 1807 collection, 'Elegiac Stanzas,' exposes the naivety of this sentiment, one of Wordsworth's cherished and foundational notions. On its own, this poem, also known as 'Peele Castle,' puts paid to the vindication of Nature's benevolence in 'Tintern Abbey.' In Wordsworth's *oeuvre*, however, it is only a momentary crisis of faith. It is commonplace to see Wordsworth in his poetry becoming more conventionally spiritual, if not so specifically religious, after 1807. In other words, in the later Wordsworth, Nature and God are more closely intertwined. And Wordsworth commits himself to the teleology of the love of Nature leading to the love of humankind, as he explores in *The Prelude*. And looking forward to *The Excursion* and the later revisions of *The Prelude*, we see that that teleology is increasingly informed by general Christian principles and theology.

In 1798, Wordsworth had experienced considerable anguish and despair; but he had never suffered a loss as great as that of February 1805: his sea-captain brother, John, drowned when his ship foundered off the Portland Bill. Wordsworth's poems

'To the Daisy' and 'I Only Looked for Pain and Grief' capture his initial devastation (*MW* 307–11). 'Elegiac Stanzas,' however, is a far more complicated response to John's death that was inspired by viewing in 1806 the painting *A Storm: Peele Castle* by Sir George Beaumont, who had become a patron of Wordsworth. As the poem explains, Wordsworth had lived briefly near Peele Castle in the summer of 1794. Beaumont's painting depicts the ruined castle standing next to stormy, tumultuous waves upon which a small ship appears in danger of capsizing. Powerfully informed by his brother's shipwreck, Wordsworth's poem develops a response to this painting that compares his pleasant experience of the actual place years before with the way Beaumont represents it in his picture. Wordsworth's use of the painting to express his grief makes 'Elegiac Stanzas' a fascinating example of *ekphrasis*, the representation of a work of art in a different medium. Wordsworth's perception of the painting's depiction becomes an emblem for the theme of the poem—the awesome power of Nature and its sublime indifference to human life. As Wordsworth writes, 'A deep distress hath humanized my Soul' (36).

The poem is 'elegiac' in more ways than one. It mourns the loss of a loved one—although, unlike traditional laments such as Spenser's 'Astrophel' (1595) or Milton's 'Lycidas' (1637), it does not specifically identify the deceased and only indirectly suggests that Beaumont, the poet's friend, 'would have been the Friend, / If he had lived, of Him, whom I deplore' (41–2). Mostly it is generally elegiac after the manner of Charlotte Smith's *Elegiac Sonnets*, which Wordsworth admired and which express great sorrow and despair. Like Gray's 'Elegy Written in a Country Churchyard,' it is elegiac also in its employment of the elegiac quatrain, an ancient form associated with feeling and that in English consists of four lines of iambic pentameter rhyming ABAB. So, as its title indicates, the poem is richly allusive in its form alone. Such attention to form is appropriate given its relationship to Beaumont's painting and Wordsworth's address to the castle within the work of art. The poem opens by making a provocative distinction between the castle and its representation even before it specifically refers to the painting. In the first stanza, Wordsworth distinguishes between his 'sight' of the actual castle and its reflection in the calm coastal water; back then, when he saw the castle, 'Thy Form was sleeping on a glassy sea' (4). The poem effectively addresses the reflection of the castle to emphasize how placid the water was then—'Whene'er I looked, thy Image still was there; / It trembled, but it never passed away' (7–8)—and to emphasize the relative perception of the castle before and after his brother's death. This 'Image' of the castle seemed permanent then, corresponding with his naive belief that 'the mighty Deep / Was even the gentlest of all gentle Things' (11–12). The poem is also an elegy for such faith.

When he considers what he would have painted then, Wordsworth does so with a touch of sarcasm directed toward his former self and his former aesthetic. The poet-as-painter would have added 'the gleam, / The light that never was, on sea or land, / The consecration, and the Poet's dream' (14–16). These lines bitterly comment upon the way in which art may alter reality—even when that reality seems true at the time. The painting he did not paint—Beaumont's painting—turns out to be more true than 'the fond delusion of my heart' (29). When he looks at the picture Beaumont has made, he praises its 'spirit' as 'well chosen' and true: 'That Hulk which labours in the deadly swell, / This rueful sky, this pageantry of fear!' (46–8). Where before he had admired the castle as 'a treasure-house, a mine / Of peaceful years,' now he sees it 'Cased in the unfeeling armour of old time,' protected and sealed off from the elements (21–2, 51). Whatever is inside that suit of armour, it is not human. Finally, unlike the Leech-Gatherer, the castle is irrelevant as a symbol because 'the Heart that lives alone, / Housed in a dream' is 'blind' happiness; people cannot live this way, 'at distance from the Kind!'—that is, from other people (53–6). The poem ends recognizing a greater truth in the painting: we are not like the castle withstanding the elements, but rather more like whoever captains the ship that is being tossed upon the waves. 'Not without hope,' the poem concludes, 'we suffer and we mourn' (60). Even though the emphasis is not on the hope, the poet is ready to face 'frequent sights of what is to be borne!,' to stand before art that reminds him of the difficulties we all must face. As an artist himself, neither will he turn away from those truths. *Poems, in Two Volumes* then concludes with Wordsworth facing the greatest challenge yet—the crisis of vision and mortality that propels the 'Intimations Ode.'

FOR FURTHER STUDY

1. Another famous example of *ekphrasis* is Keats's 'Ode on a Grecian Urn.' Compare the way the two poets describe the visual artifact in order to express the respective themes of each poem. How does each poem relate to the other work of art? How do these poems use the other medium to comment upon poetry and its relationship to other artistic forms?

2. Compare Wordsworth's treatment of personal loss and grief in 'Elegiac Stanzas' with his sonnet 'Surprized by Joy' (1815) on the death of his four-year-old daughter Catherine in 1812 (*MW* 334). Consider the formal implications of developing these themes in elegiac quatrains versus a sonnet, particularly as the sonnet has a predetermined structure that Wordsworth follows perfectly. How does the formal structure relate to the expression of grief in each poem? (I believe 'Surprized by Joy' to be the finest sonnet Wordsworth ever wrote.)

Approaching the 'Great Ode'

The final poem in the 1807 volume is the one that made Wordsworth's reputation for the nineteenth century. First published simply as 'Ode,' Wordsworth later gave it the title 'Ode. Intimations of Immortality from Recollections of Early Childhood' for his 1815 collection, in which it also appears last. The placement suggests Wordsworth's sense of the Ode as the ultimate statement in these collections (although he downplayed its significance in later collections). Sometimes referred to as 'the Intimations Ode,' 'the Immortality Ode,' or even 'the Great Ode,' this poem is notoriously difficult but impossible to ignore: Wordsworth's friend and admirer Henry Crabb Robinson, for example, remarked that the poem made him feel 'ridiculous' because he was 'unable to explain precisely what I admired' (quoted in Gilchrist 386). And yet, in 1856, Ralph Waldo Emerson called the poem 'the high-water mark which the intellect has reached in this age' (quoted in Gill, *Victorians* 14). At the same time, despite the great distinction bestowed upon it over the past 200 years, most readers and critics admit at least some difficulty actually appreciating it; critic Francis Jeffrey found it 'unintelligible' (see Chapter 4), and Coleridge objected to Wordsworth's portrayal of the child in lines 110–19. A long-standing critical tradition holds that the

'Intimations Ode' is important but problematic and, according to some critics, flawed.

The difficulty comes from the impression many readers have that the poem does not hold together as well as some of Wordsworth's other poems. It is a long irregular ode that has neither a fixed lyrical form nor the syllabic regularity of blank verse. Moreover, it rhymes in varying line-lengths and schemes that result in a syncopated effect that is off-putting to today's ears. We are used to seeing Wordsworth work either in blank verse or in fixed stanzas. The poem becomes all the more disorienting as its opening stanzas develop a Wordsworthian crisis of faith that is particularly striking in the 1807 context. After many charming lyrics about butterflies, various birds, rainbows, and even a playful kitten, Wordsworth closes the book with a poem that starkly admits 'The things which I have seen I now can see no more' and that 'there hath passed away a glory from the earth' (9, 18). The first section of the poem concludes with despairing questions rather than the lyrical insights derived from nature we have come to expect: 'Whither is fled the visionary gleam? / Where is it now, the glory and the dream?' (56–7). Wordsworth insists that he still hears, sees, and feels the joy all around him, but he laments the loss of precisely the kind of vision he seems to have gained from experiences described in such poems as 'Tintern Abbey' and the daffodils poem. We expect the poem, then, to move toward a resolution of this crisis, and having studied the 1805 *Prelude*, which he completed after writing the opening four stanzas of the Ode, we certainly expect that he will find recourse in a previous experience that will revivify his imagination. But, instead, the poem becomes philosophical and didactic—in other words, it does not sound at all like the Wordsworth of 'Tintern Abbey.'

Every reader of the poem has to account for the sense that it is ostensibly two poems: Wordsworth wrote the first four stanzas in 1802 as an attempt at a Pindaric ode, in which the first two stanzas function as the strophe and antistrophe and the longer final two as the epode; he returned to the poem and completed the rest of it in 1804. Even if we did not know these facts, we would discern nonetheless a shift between the first-person 'I' of the first four stanzas and the more universal, philosophical-sounding first-person plurals ('our,' 'we') and third-person subjects of most of the rest of the poem—that is, until the final stanza. The development of such a quintessential issue for Wordsworth as the 'visionary gleam' perceived in the world around him seems unlike him.

What emerges in critical discussions is the awareness of not only two separately composed sections but basically three movements: the first four stanzas from 1802, lines 1–57, comprise the first movement; the rest of the poem, written in 1804, provides a response to the first movement in a second movement of four stanzas, lines 58–131; and a final, third movement of three stanzas, goes from line 132 until the end. The second movement addresses the problem by suggesting that 'the visionary gleam' has not fled, but that 'we' grow away from it in our progress from birth to death. These stanzas emphasize the visionary nature of children through their spiritual proximity to heaven, where the soul has pre-existence: at our birth, we come 'trailing clouds of glory . . . / From God, who is our home' (64–5). In the fifth, sixth, and seventh stanzas, Wordsworth explains that the child has some sense of that pre-existence; but through socialization and maturity—'Shades of the prison-house begin to close / Upon the growing Boy'—eventually the adult loses the vision as it fades 'into the light of common day' (67–8, 76). The 'Intimations Ode,' then, engages themes that compare usefully with Blake's *Songs of Innocence and of Experience*.

A definitive reading of the poem remains elusive, but Lionel Trilling's comes closest in the simple assertion that it is 'about growing up' (151). And while Wordsworth's vision of adulthood is not as grim as Blake's, coming from him it feels more depressing. A particularly troubling stanza, lines 77–84, presents a view of Earth as a 'homely Nurse' that contrasts sharply with the usual way he presents Nature: in 'Tintern Abbey,' for instance, Wordsworth describes 'nature and the language of the sense' as 'the nurse, / The guide, the guardian of my heart, and soul / Of all my moral being' (109–12). Here, we might ask if this portrayal of Mother Nature represents the same force:

> Earth fills her lap with pleasures of her own;
> Yearnings she hath in her own natural kind,
> And, even with something of a Mother's mind,
>   And no unworthy aim,

> The homely Nurse doth all she can
> To make her Foster-child, her Inmate Man,
> Forget the glories he hath known,
> And that imperial palace whence he came.

These lines suggest complicity on Nature's part in the socialization of the child—indeed a mortification of the child—and the degradation of the child's visionary power. Wordsworth explained later that his use of 'the notion of pre-existence' was not so much a spiritual conviction as a poetic device (see *MW* 714). Here, most uncharacteristically, he uses physical nature as a metaphor for mortality, devoid of the spiritual immanence so frequently celebrated in his other poetry. The physical, material world is associated with mortality and with something like philosophical necessity and thus contributes to the diminution of the 'intimations of immortality' the child enjoys.

The next stanza, lines 85–107, provides specific examples of the child's socialization through imitation of adult behavior and adult concerns. This is how the child learns to be an adult—'As if his whole vocation / Were endless imitation.' And then the next stanza, lines 108–31, seems to reverse the poem's progress to adulthood with the paean to childhood that so annoyed Coleridge. So, in what sense may the child be the 'best Philosopher'? The opening lines of the stanza recognize the paradox of proportion: the child's 'exterior semblance doth belie / Thy Soul's immensity.' In the literal sense of philosophy as the love of knowledge, Wordsworth's claim is not as hyperbolic as it sounds, for we all know that children are like sponges when it comes to new experiences. But Wordsworth complicates his meaning by denying the empirical elements that we understand to be essential to development: the child is an 'Eye among the blind, / That, deaf and silent, read'st the eternal deep, / Haunted for ever by the eternal mind.' Philosophers naturally cannot accept a conception of the child as the keeper of a Platonic truth, as possessing an inherent rational perfection that defies empiricism— the child does not empirically experience the world in a Lockean sense but 'read'st' and thus knows a Platonic truth that will eventually fade. Wordsworth likely is being deliberately provocative of Enlightenment epistemology in favor of something like Christian transcendence. But it is a transcendence that is weighted down and oppressed by the mundane concerns of adulthood, what Wordsworth calls 'custom'; it is 'Heavy as frost.'

As the poem moves into its final movement, Wordsworth is called upon to provide some sort of happy ending, some sense of 'abundant recompense.' And here it behooves the reader to think back to the beginning of the poem and to consider how well the conclusion of the poem responds to its opening. The first four stanzas of the poem offer a perspective unique to the poet (or a poet) and its concern is rooted in a crisis of creativity and of the imagination. The poem's second movement has universalized this concern, making it common to all human beings and a matter of the soul. In the next long stanza, lines 132–70, the poet claims to be grateful for the memory of having once been in touch with a sense of immortality. As Stuart Sperry points out, memory is no longer 'reconstitutive,' as it is in 'Tintern Abbey,' but a powerful memory of what he has lost: it is 'the operation of a memory of a highly limited but now vitally significant kind' (41). This may be difficult to swallow; but it is 'Those shadowy recollections' that, as a compelling reading by Anya Taylor suggests, that make us dissatisfied with the limits of mortality and make us believe that we have souls. The poem does look forward to the realization of an immortal life beyond 'Our noisy years' of mortal existence. The conclusion of this stanza reassures us that we can still access that feeling of transcendence:

> Hence, in a season of calm weather,
> Though inland far we be,
> Our Souls have sight of that immortal sea
> Which brought us hither,
> Can in a moment travel thither,
> And see the Children sport upon the shore,
> And hear the mighty waters rolling evermore.

While this may be a comforting assertion of immortality, these lines do not specifically resolve the crisis of the beginning of the poem. The peculiar difficulty of the 'Intimations Ode' is that Wordsworth turns to a resolution that stands counter to so much of his other work—particularly, as we have seen, the 1805 *Prelude*. An important reading by Florence G. Marsh points out the poem's internal contradiction between its expressions of faith in a 'divinity within,' which sounds a lot like the Wordsworth of 'Tintern Abbey' and *The Prelude*, and a 'divine life best known before birth and after death' (230). Wordsworth usually celebrates immanence instead of transcendence. Taylor's reading suggests that a Christian reading—not a Wordsworthian reading—is necessary to reconcile this problem. A more conventionally Christian reading of the poem—whether or not Wordsworth intended it in 1802–1807—certainly helps to understand why the poem was so appealing to nineteenth-century readers, particularly those disturbed by their own crises of faith. One way to appreciate the 'Intimations Ode' is to read Christian transcendence against Wordsworthian immanence. In other words, the 'Intimations Ode' invites us to read it against the grain of everything else we know about Wordsworth.

But it is also possible to appreciate the poem not as a carefully reasoned philosophical position. The poem ends with acceptance that the 'visionary gleam' has been replaced with 'a sober colouring from an eye / That hath kept watch o'er man's mortality' (200–1) and with the wonderfully enigmatic conclusion that 'To me the meanest flower that blows can give / Thoughts that do often lie too deep for tears' (205–6). Perhaps we end the poem back on familiar Wordsworth territory, with a sense of the 'still, sad music of humanity' (92). So, the image of the invisible power operating upon the flower and inspiring thought shows Wordsworth perhaps not wholly committing to transcendence over immanence. Peter J. Manning suggests that the 'Intimations Ode' 'exploits the resonances of Christian faith without committing itself to belief, to the conviction that would lessen its human uncertainty' (538). In other words, doubt is perhaps more true to human experience than certainty. Perhaps the whole poem is nothing more than lyrical speculation about 'the faith that looks through death, / In years that bring the philosophic mind' (188–9). Wordsworth certainly is free to indulge 'the philosophic mind' without committing wholly to a philosophical or theological system. As Stuart Curran reminds us, the conclusion of the 'Intimations Ode' is also the conclusion of *Poems, in Two Volumes* and as such brings together all the themes of the book—'all the multiple contraries'—'youth and age, desire and experience, success and failure.' Moreover, the final lines, Curran suggests, 'deliberately return us to the opening poem of volume 1, "To the

Daisy," now reconceptualized in almost cosmic terms' (235). In this way, the volume comes full circle.

The 'Intimations Ode,' still, is something of an anomaly. In it, Wordsworth advances ideas that we cannot find elsewhere in his poetry, especially in poetry of this period. One of my students said once that she felt Wordsworth was 'trying on' the philosopher's robes and suggested that Wordsworth may be attempting to impersonate Coleridge and his philosophical speculations and more conventional Christian beliefs. Coleridge indeed is a presence in the 'Intimations Ode,' and this provides yet another way of approaching it. Its composition history has more than a few interesting wrinkles. The 1802 Pindaric ode was written as a response to Coleridge's despair at losing his poetical powers, a despair that may have infected Wordsworth as well. As Paul Magnuson, Gene W. Ruoff, Lucy Newlyn, and others have shown, the idiosyncrasies of Wordsworth's 'Intimations Ode' likely derive from its being written in dialogue with Coleridge. Ruoff's study *Wordsworth and Coleridge: The Making of the Major Lyrics, 1802–1804* is particularly ingenious in its organization according to the stages of this dialogue: it opens with a chapter on the 1802 version of the ode, then Ruoff shows how Coleridge's unrelentingly dark verse letter to Sara Hutchinson, written shortly after his reading of Wordsworth's ode, is a specific response to it. Coleridge's poem would become known as 'Dejection: An Ode'; but before it appeared in print, Wordsworth responded to it with 'The Leech-Gatherer' and the revised version, 'Resolution and Independence'; Coleridge's first published version of 'Dejection' appeared in a newspaper in October of that year—coincidentally on the day of Wordsworth's wedding and Coleridge's own wedding anniversary. This version is addressed to Wordsworth as 'Edmund' instead of to Sara. (Coleridge would republish the poem, with 'Lady' now in place of 'Edmund,' in 1817.) The final version of the 'Intimations Ode,' then, is the conclusion of this poetic dialogue and can be read alongside the other texts with illuminating results, showing how Wordsworth's 'Great Ode' extensively engages his friend and collaborator—especially since *The Recluse* failed to materialize and Wordsworth's major effort toward it, *The Excursion* of 1814, seems so deliberately defiant of Coleridge's intentions for the great philosophical poem. The public dialogue between them would continue, as we will see in the next chapter, but the 'Intimations Ode' read in relation to 'Dejection' feels like the conclusion of the great collaboration and marks the end of their private poetic exchange.

FOR FURTHER STUDY

1. The 'Intimations Ode' shares with 'Tintern Abbey' the theme of memory, so you might find it helpful to compare the two poems—particularly in regard to 'abundant recompense' for what the poet feels he has lost. In this respect is the 'Intimations Ode' more or less convincing than 'Tintern Abbey'?

2. In later versions of the 'Ode,' Wordsworth replaced the Latin epigraph with the final four lines of 'My Heart Leaps Up'— how might this affect your reading of the 'Ode'?

3. What is the 'timely utterance' in line 23? Trilling thinks it is a reference to 'Resolution and Independence'; Carl Woodring suggests that it is 'My Heart Leaps Up' (91). But such extra-textual explanations require too much outside knowledge—is the 'timely utterance' a reference to something within the poem, in this particular stanza?

4. Wordsworth wrote 'Elegiac Stanzas' after completing the 'Intimations Ode,' so what does his placement of 'Elegiac Stanzas' before the Ode in *Poems, in Two Volumes* suggest about the way the poems may relate to one another?

CHAPTER 4

CRITICAL RECEPTION AND
PUBLISHING HISTORY

In 1801, Wordsworth's brother John acknowledged, 'I do not think [Wordsworth's] poetry will become popular for some time to come' because 'it certainly does not suit the present taste' (Woof 98). One of the reasons for focusing on the poetry of 'the great decade' is that after 1807, as a result of his work's critical reception, Wordsworth began a lifelong process of revising his poems in accordance with the criticisms he received and with an eye increasingly focused on his reputation and posterity. While he believed in 'creating the taste' for his poetry, he could not help collaborating somewhat with what he believed the public wanted. He was ambitious certainly, but he was also a professional writer trying to earn a living. For example, his 1815 collection shows the influence of the 1807 critics; and his 1820 collection reveals more significant revisions—likely as the result of Coleridge's critical remarks in his *Biographia Literaria* (1817).

The period from 1807, the publication year for *Poems, in Two Volumes*, to 1850, the year of Wordsworth's death, is generally acknowledged to be, as Harold Bloom puts it, 'the longest dying of a major poetic genius in history' (*Western* 250). While readers should be aware of this view, we should also keep in mind that Wordsworth's literary activity during the same period gradually brought him the success that preserved his reputation for the rest of the nineteenth century. But it was a difficult slog for the poet. Shortly after *Poems, in Two Volumes* appeared in print, Wordsworth wrote to Lady Beaumont, expressing his anxiety about publication and doubts about the book's reception:

> It is an awful truth, that there neither is, nor can be, any genuine enjoyment of Poetry among nineteen out of twenty of those persons who live, or wish to live, in the broad light of the world—among those who either are, or are striving to make

themselves, people of consideration in society. This is a truth, and an awful one, because to be incapable of a feeling of Poetry in my sense of the word is to be without love of human nature and reverence for God. (*Middle Years* 1: 146)

Then, as today, 'genuine' lovers of poetry were hard to come by perhaps; but Wordsworth's poetry, especially after *Lyrical Ballads* (1798–1800) and before *The River Duddon* (1820), was notably unpalatable to the public. However, the fact that Wordsworth could express this in a letter to Lady Beaumont, the wife of his new friend and benefactor Sir George Beaumont, shows that he was gaining the admiration of a select and elite few. As his and his family's relationship with Coleridge became increasingly strained, Wordsworth found a valuable new literary associate and 'kindred spirit' in Walter Scott (Gill, *Life* 217). In the first decade of the nineteenth century, the poet also strengthened his friendship with Robert Southey, with whom he had previously had tensions.

Southey had come around, asserting that the *Lyrical Ballads* 'will one day be regarded as the finest poems in our language' (Woof 121). At first, however, Southey was among those who failed to appreciate the 'experiments' of the edition of *Lyrical Ballads*—despite the fact that he was friendly with Wordsworth and brother-in-law to Coleridge when it first appeared. Southey's harshest remarks are directed toward 'The Idiot Boy' and 'The Rime of the Ancyent Marinere,' although he reserves singular praise for 'Tintern Abbey.' His review particularly stung Wordsworth, who feared it would adversely affect sales. Wordsworth wrote in a letter, 'I care little for the praise of any other professional critic, but as it may help me to pudding' (*Early Years* 268). It is important to remember that Wordsworth and Coleridge needed the money, so they hoped for as many favorable reviews as possible. Although they were mixed, the reviews of the first edition of *Lyrical Ballads* were just positive enough and were in fact the best reviews Wordsworth would receive for more than 20 years. Despite initial slow sales, the first edition sold out within a year, warranting a second edition. After receiving an annuity from the Wedgwood family in 1798, Coleridge no longer needed the money and lost interest in the project, but Wordsworth continued to need to sell books. This explains a lot about the publication history of *Lyrical Ballads*—why Wordsworth took control of the project, why he excluded 'Christabel,' why he wrote dismissively of 'The Ancient Mariner' in the 1800 note, and why he composed and continued to expand the Preface.

THE LAKE SCHOOL: POETRY AND POLITICS

It was that famous Preface that sharpened critical knives, appearing to present itself as a literary manifesto. After the 1802 edition, critics began to recognize 'a new school of poetry' and Wordsworth as 'the senior professor in this Parnassian college' (Woof 144). Francis Jeffrey, reviewing Southey's *Thalaba* in 1802, identifies Wordsworth as the leader of a new 'sect of poets' and Southey as 'one of its chief champions and apostles' (Woof 153). He here includes Coleridge and Charles Lamb as well. Denying their originality, Jeffrey distinguishes strands of imitation and attendant characteristics: from Rousseau they have derived 'antisocial principles, and distempered sensibility'; from German poets Kotzebue and Schiller 'simplicity and energy'; from Cowper 'homeliness and harshness'; and from English poet Ambrose Philips, whose pastorals were memorably ridiculed by John Gay for their simplicity, they have derived what Jeffrey sarcastically calls '*innocence*' (154). Although he had been 'enchanted' with *Lyrical Ballads* when it first appeared, Jeffrey finds their aesthetic of simplicity to belie a more depraved 'rejection of art altogether' and the subsequent 'debasement of all those feelings which poetry is designed to communicate' (Woof 58, 156).

Poems, in Two Volumes made matters worse. An exasperated writer for the *Critical Review*, admitting the failure of the journal's previous attempts at 'bringing him back to his senses,' finally exclaims, 'we fear that the mind of Mr. W. has been too long accustomed to the enervating debauchery of taste for us to entertain much hope of his recovery' (Woof 172–3).

In his review of the 1807 collection, Jeffrey, rising once more in opposition, famously delineates Wordsworth, Southey, and Coleridge as the 'Lake' school, 'a certain brotherhood of poets, who have haunted for some years about the Lakes of Cumberland' (Woof 185). Again, the complaints circle around Wordsworth's style and diction: he and 'his friends' 'write as they do, upon principle and system; and it evidently costs them much pains to keep *down* to the standard which they have proposed to themselves' (Woof 189). But also, Jeffrey objects to Wordsworth's manner 'of connecting his most lofty, tender, or impassioned conceptions, with objects and incidents, which the greater part of his readers will probably persist in thinking low, silly, or uninteresting' (Woof 189). It is an eviscerating review to be sure. Although he predictably praises the more traditional sonnets, Jeffrey clearly sees Wordsworth as a 'rebel' who must be symbolically executed as 'a wholesome warning' to other poets whom he hopes will 'be the means of restoring to that antient [*sic*] and venerable code its due honour and authority' (201). Thus the review ends on a reactionary note that strangely echoes in poetics the political ideology of Burke's attack on the French Revolution all the way back in 1790.

Despite great differences in their writing styles, Wordsworth, Coleridge, and Southey continued to be associated—to the detriment of all three. In his 1813 poetic satire, on the model of Pope, *English Bards and Scotch Reviewers*, the young Lord Byron places his inveterate enemy Southey chief among the new poets, making Wordsworth 'the dull disciple of thy school' (175). By 1814, the Lake Poets were generally known as such. In 1818, Hazlitt made it clear that Wordsworth 'is at the head' of 'the Lake school of poetry' and that the poetic principles of this school derive from 'those sentiments and opinions which produced' the French Revolution—controversial principles indeed for a post-Waterloo political climate in which the French Revolution appeared to be an abject failure. Their enemies were able thus to paint the Lake poets as subversive to those English values and traditions that had carried the day.

The three continued to be associated not just for poetical reasons but political ones as well. Although he still lived in the Lake District, Southey became an increasingly public figure. Turning his back on his previous views, Southey had gone on to become a spokesman for conservative politics, particularly in his writing for the *Quarterly Review*, earning for himself a government pension and then, in 1813, the position of Poet Laureate. Coleridge began writing for Tory periodicals. Around the same time, Wordsworth, who had always been considered something of an eccentric rustic recluse, controversially accepted a job as

Distributor of Stamps for his county, effectively serving as a tax collector. For the younger generation of poets who had admired Wordsworth's iconoclastic break with tradition, this was a major sell-out of his principles. But Wordsworth was desperate to provide for his family, having recently moved them into the elegant house at Rydal Mount; he wanted an actual job, as opposed to becoming a government shill. According to Leigh Hunt, this position 'marked [Wordsworth] as government property' (Woof 337). More damaging was his dedication of *The Excursion* to Lord Lonsdale, who, to be fair, had been long associated with the family and who had helped Wordsworth immensely. The dedication was seen as a turn toward Tory politics, and Wordsworth was seen as a turncoat. In response to the gesture, mocking Wordsworth's place 'at Lord Lonsdale's table,' Byron described the other poet as a 'poetical charlatan and political parasite' (1044). The young Percy Bysshe Shelley previously had admired Wordsworth, despite his association with Southey, for maintaining in his poverty 'the integrity of his independence' (Woof 319). However, as Mary Shelley notes, upon opening *The Excursion*, she and Shelley immediately deduced from the dedication that 'He is a slave' (25).

Generally, Wordsworth does become more conservative in his later years. But we should resist oversimplifying his politics. For example, in 1809, he wrote a pamphlet on the *Convention of Cintra* that denounced the agreement, negotiated by Arthur Wellesley, the future Duke of Wellington, that allowed the defeated French army to depart the Iberian Peninsula and return home. Wordsworth celebrates the Spanish and Portuguese nationals who resisted Napoleon's armies and who called upon England to help them, and harshly condemns the British government for its betrayal. Here, he takes on Milton's mantle as polemicist and pamphleteer instead of epic poet. Although it did not sell well, it earned Wordsworth more favorable notices than he was accustomed to receive for his poetry. For instance, even when his patriotic 'Thanksgiving Ode' (1816) appeared in celebration of the British victory over Napoleon, unfriendly reviewers, while approving the poet's sentiments, continue to attack his simple language and to needle him with the appellation of 'Lake Poet.' Still, readers who admire the humanitarian principles of such early poems as 'The Old Cumberland Beggar,' 'The Female Vagrant,' or 'Goody

Blake and Harry Gill' are not going to be greatly pleased with the values the elderly Wordsworth expresses in such poems as *Sonnets upon the Punishment of Death* (1842) or *Sonnets Dedicated to Liberty and Order* (1845).

In addition to harsh reviews, the poetry was relentlessly parodied in attacks upon the pejoratively labeled 'Lake School.' The parodies attest to certain recognizable stylistic peculiarities requisite for such satire to work. Contemporary parodies of Wordsworth range from easy burlesque jabs, such as one called 'The Baby's Debut' that ridicules Wordsworth's simple language by implying that his poems might as well have been written by children, to more sophisticated stylistic satire, such as James Hogg's 'The Stranger,' which combines simple diction with elaborate, long, and pretentious Miltonic sentences. An early parody that stung Wordsworth personally was Peter Bayley's 'The Fisherman's Wife' (1803), which renders ridiculous Wordsworth's rural characters and ordinary subjects but also his practice of using simple diction within rhyming stanzas, pointing out the seeming incongruity of eschewing artificial diction while preserving other formal qualities of poetry: in the poem a child cries,

> Mother! dear Mother! cease to weep!
> My father will return anon,
> At eve he'll come: beyond the lake
> He waits secure, or else to take
> His fish to market he is gone. (Kent 50)

What is funny about the parody is how the deliberate construction of a stanza pattern, particularly the altering of syntax to rhyme, culminates in fish-mongering, which is the kind of unpoetical subject many critics attacked Wordsworth's poetry for having. But at the heart of the parody is also the fundamental stylistic issue in Wordsworth. Similarly, in his satirical poem *The Simpliciad* (1808), the Reverend Richard Mant attacked Wordsworth, Southey, and Coleridge for their 'perverted taste' (*LBRW* 382). In his comic masterpiece, *Don Juan* (1819), Byron derisively puts the three Lake poets together in direct opposition to the three greatest English poets in his estimation:

> Thou shalt believe in Milton, Dryden, Pope;
> Thou shalt not set up Wordsworth, Coleridge, Southey;

Because the first is crazed beyond all hope,
The second drunk, the third so quaint and mouthey.
. . . (429)

Byron, whose taste in literature was fundamentally conservative, found the Lake poets as representing a new and repugnant direction for poetry. As a satirist, therefore, he was happy to lampoon them. Moreover, the publication of Wordsworth's long comic ballad of redemption *Peter Bell* (1819), itself almost a parody of 'The Rime of the Ancient Mariner,' turned out to be a disaster due to renewed critical drubbing exacerbated by John Hamilton Reynolds's burlesque *Peter Bell, A Lyrical Ballad*, based on the meter of 'The Idiot Boy,' published the week before Wordsworth's poem appeared. Other parodies would follow, including one called *The Dead Asses*. Shelley's *Peter Bell the Third*, which was written in 1819 but not published until 1839, attacks Wordsworth for his turncoat politics, hypocrisy, egotism, didacticism, and general dullness. While the parodies actually did boost sales and increase public curiosity, they did not boost Wordsworth's reputation. As one critic noted, 'Humorous, and we regret to add, malevolent criticism has been busy with Mr. Wordsworth's poetry' (Woof 795).

SALVAGING A DAMAGED CAREER

'This will never do,' Francis Jeffrey exasperatedly declares, opening his damning 1814 review of *The Excursion*, the most ambitious work Wordsworth had published—or would ever publish in his lifetime. *The Excursion* brought to a head the critical controversies boiling since *Lyrical Ballads*. As late as 1821, Byron was still harping on what many agreed to be the poem's excessive length and self-indulgence: in *Don Juan*, he mocks 'A drowsy frowzy poem, call'd the "Excursion" / Writ in a manner which is my aversion' (514). The reception of *The Excursion* is the lowest point certainly of Wordsworth's career. The nine-book, 9,000-line poem, which William Hazlitt described as dropping 'still-born from the press' ('Mr Wordsworth' 167), is difficult to describe and difficult to appreciate. It involves the interaction of four characters—the Poet, the Wanderer, the Solitary, and the Pastor—and their discussion of various issues, occasionally interrupted by description of the Lake District, where it is set, and by interpolated tales. The characters debate despondency, optimism, stoicism, utilitarianism, religion, government, and education. The poem ultimately validates the perspective of the Pastor and his values of home, family, and community—the Wordsworthian *philia* in action. To us today, the poem seems more Christian than most of the major works of the Romantic period; but Wordsworth's contemporary readers were uncomfortable with the generic spirituality of the poem and the absence of Jesus Christ and the Gospels (see Woof 424). When William Blake read the Preface, particularly its 'Prospectus' to *The Recluse*, he believed it induced a bowel complaint that nearly killed him (Bentley 312). *The Excursion* prompted a more positive reassessment of Wordsworth's career in the liberal newspaper *The Champion* in 1814; its review concluded that Wordsworth is 'of too high an order' to be 'a popular poet': 'he writes for men who reflect as deeply as himself' (Woof 344).

Some of those 'who reflect as deeply' were to be the second generation of Romantics. These writers, who were less attached to traditional literary values than Jeffrey and other critics, began to rehabilitate somewhat Wordsworth's reputation; and, even when they did not always praise him, they could not deny his importance. Leigh Hunt, who had poked fun at him in an earlier version of his *Feast of the Poets*, takes his genius more seriously in the lengthy notes to the 1815 edition of the poem. In 1814, just prior to Jeffrey's attack, William Hazlitt favorably reviewed *The Excursion* in a long three-part essay in Hunt's newspaper *The Examiner*. Although occasionally malicious, Hazlitt is among the first incisive readers of Wordsworth. Reviewing *The Excursion*, Hazlitt downplays the controversies over Wordsworth's style and looks more deeply into the poet's idiosyncratic philosophy: he writes, 'The power of his mind preys upon itself. It is as if there were nothing but himself and the universe. He lives in the busy solitude of his own heart; in the deep silence of thought' (Woof 371). The younger Romantics' perception of Wordsworth as an isolated figure is what attracted them—and what made them rebel against him. Wordsworth was appealing to this generation precisely because he seemed to them, in his early poetry, to be a rebel; but he also was a measuring stick for their own ambitions, making him not only an influence but an object of critical scrutiny. The young John Keats, for instance, greatly admired *The Excursion*, calling it one of the 'things to rejoice at in this Age' (70). Keats's letters show him thinking about whether or not Wordsworth will supersede Milton, concluding that Wordsworth has a greater insight 'into the human heart' than Milton (125). Keats's most famous observation about Wordsworth derives from comparing him with Shakespeare. Keats finds that his allegiance is with Shakespeare, 'the camelion [*sic*] Poet,' the artist whose self, character, and identity disappear in the work; this Keats contrasts with 'the wordsworthian [*sic*] or egotistical sublime; which is a thing per se and stands alone' (194). Keats's phrase 'egotistical sublime' is apt in the sense that Wordsworth's poetry does frequently marvel at the majesty of its own subjectivity. Wordsworth's peers recognized this. For example, Henry Crabb Robinson recorded in his diary a conversation in which Lamb asserted that Wordsworth 'does not, like Shakespeare, become everything he pleases, but forces the reader to submit to his individual feelings' (Woof 302). In his short career, Keats remained ambivalent, for certainly his poetry contains much of the 'egotistical sublime.' Keats likely would have continued to define himself in relation to Wordsworth's presentation of the self had he lived.

Although he was critical at times, the Romantic poet most receptive to Wordsworth is Shelley. Shelley's poems of 1816 such as 'Alastor; or, The Spirit in Solitude,' 'Hymn to Intellectual Beauty' and 'Mont Blanc' have deep Wordsworthian resonances—even as 'Alastor' and the sonnet 'To Wordsworth' criticize respectively the Wordsworthian solitary and, in Shelley's view, the politically compromised poet. As Mary Shelley apologetically remarks in her note to *Peter Bell the Third*, 'No man ever admired Wordsworth's poetry more;—he read it perpetually' ('Note' 357). The evidence certainly supports this. Shelley, in contrast to Keats's stated preference for the Shakespearean approach, embraced the concept of the 'egotistical sublime' but wanted to put it more powerfully to use as a revolutionary political and philosophical mode of inquiry than he believed Wordsworth was interested in doing. Despite his disappointment in *The Excursion*, Shelley's enthusiasm for Wordsworth spread to Byron, who complained, 'Shelley, when I was in Switzerland, used to dose me with Wordsworth physic even to nausea' (quoted in Medwin 237). And yet Byron's 1816 works *Manfred* and *Childe Harold, Canto the Third* show the influence of Wordsworth—so much so that Wordsworth himself complained to the poet Thomas Moore of Byron's plagiarism in *Childe Harold*, insisting, according to Moore, that 'Tintern Abbey is the source of it all' (Moore 355).

Unlike Byron, the instant celebrity, Wordsworth was a still-struggling author in mid-career, often the object of critical scorn and public ridicule. Wordsworth in his 50-year career likely never sold as many books as Byron did in his 10-year career. But Wordsworth persisted with a clear aim toward poetic immortality. He began to regard himself as having the staying power of one of the great poets. For his 1815 *Poems*, Wordsworth began classifying his poetry as pertaining to such categories as childhood, affections, fancy, imagination, and sentiment and reflection. He revised his canon again for a new four-volume edition of 1820, indicating that he saw all of his poems not chronologically but as a complete *oeuvre*. As Gill points out, this revision and reorganization was 'fresh composition' for Wordsworth, just as emotionally stressful and physically demanding as writing the poems originally (*Life* 337). He would tinker with these categories and would reorder the poems, incorporating new ones, until the end of his life. All the while, he also continued to work on *The Prelude*, even as he realized *The Recluse* was never going to materialize. He decided to save his poetic autobiography for posterity.

Significantly, just as he was collecting his works, he also began to salvage his career with new poetry. The 1820 sonnet sequence *The River Duddon* came just at the right time for Wordsworth, for its publication prompted significant critical re-evaluations of Wordsworth's poetry. This series of sonnets became for many years afterwards among his most appreciated works; its reviews are a marked contrast from those Wordsworth's publications had received the year before, though most seem apologetic for commending such an unpopular writer as Wordsworth. The *European Magazine* remarked,

His poetry may not be the most popular in the present day: it may be less frequently quoted, than that of some among his contemporaries, in crowded drawing-rooms, and less admired in fashionable circles: but we believe he is again regaining his ground in public estimation. (Woof 766–7)

Ever since the 1807 collection, critics had responded particularly favorably to Wordsworth's sonnets; and the success of *The River Duddon* justified his prolific practice of the form. With the publication of his series on the Church of England, *Ecclesiastical Sonnets*, in 1822, Wordsworth—after nearly 30 years—was finally a success in terms of his reputation. Ironically, that success came upon the emergence of two aspects of Wordsworth that may seem alien to us today: the highly formal mechanics of the sonnet and the celebration of tradition and religious institutions. Indeed, for most of the rest of the nineteenth century, his shorter poems were the most admired, although the Victorians generally deemed *The Excursion* superior to *The Prelude*—an evaluation reversed by most twentieth-century readers. Even while alive, he became himself an institution, if always somewhat iconoclastic. Although he would never sell as well as Byron, Southey, Felicia Hemans, or Thomas Moore, he was assured of having new editions always in print and for sale. In 1835, he felt certain that 'Posterity will settle all accounts justly' (*Later Years* 3: 25). When Southey died in 1843, Wordsworth was able to accept the position of Poet Laureate under Queen Victoria—on the condition that he would not have to write on command.

COLERIDGE ON WORDSWORTH

The most significant contemporary commentator on Wordsworth is of course Coleridge, whose relationship with Wordsworth was complicated early on by his sense of inferiority. As the two poets were beginning to collaborate, Coleridge wrote to Joseph Cottle, publisher of the first edition of *Lyrical Ballads*, 'I feel myself a *little man by his* side' (*Letters* 1: 325). While the relationship proved fruitful for Wordsworth's composition, it, combined with Coleridge's personal travails, stunted Coleridge's. He was unable to conceive of himself as a poet in relation to Wordsworth and Southey: in 1800, he announced, 'I abandon Poetry altogether—I leave the higher & deeper Kinds to Wordsworth, the delightful, popular & simply dignified to Southey; & reserve for myself the honorable attempt to make others feel and understand their writings, as they deserve to be felt and understood' (*Letters* 1: 623). Eventually, even as Coleridge conceded Wordsworth's superiority in poetry, he was not prepared to yield in the arenas of philosophy and literary criticism. When the Preface to *Lyrical*

Ballads appeared, Coleridge claimed it was 'half a child of my own Brain,' while suspecting that 'there is a radical Difference in theoretical opinions respecting Poetry' (*Letters* 2: 830–1). The 1815 publication of Wordsworth's collected *Poems*—along with a new preface and another reprint of the Preface to *Lyrical Ballads*—spurred a voluminous response from Coleridge in his masterpiece of literary autobiography, *Biographia Literaria* (1817). Coleridge had never been satisfied with Wordsworth's critical writing, finding it in frequent contradiction to Wordsworth's practice; the new preface irritated him further by taking up issues that Coleridge felt he had already defined—such as particularly the distinction between fancy and imagination (see *MW* 630–6, *Biographia* 1: 304–6). Generally, Coleridge wanted to set the record straight, devoting chapters 4 and 14 to discussion of *Lyrical Ballads* and the bulk of volume two, chapters 17 to 22, to an assessment of Wordsworth's poetry.

Throughout the *Biographia Literaria*, Coleridge attests to Wordsworth's genius and his supreme importance among contemporary writers. But having a generally more sophisticated philosophical mind than Wordsworth does, he means to show how the two differ in their theories about literature in many respects. Coleridge's view of poetry is essentialist, that it ought to be based on principles and on *a priori* truths. Wordsworth, Coleridge finds, bases too much of his poetry on experience and observation, and thus seems to bear too many traces of empiricism, which for Coleridge, after studying Kant, was no longer sufficient. We might think of it today in terms of Wordsworth's poetry having a tendency toward realism that Coleridge finds too matter-of-fact. Or, to put it another way, Coleridge is skeptical of Wordsworth's portrayal of rustic people and their diction because this choice is determined by the experience of such people instead of by the desire to express an *a priori* truth about human nature (see *Biographia* 2: 52–3). Coleridge does not want poetry to represent facts as much as truths. Moreover, Wordsworth's representation of rustic people and simple language is not even essential to Wordsworth's own practice, and his claims to adapt to poetry 'a selection of the real language of men,' when adapted, results in a common language that is finally not particular enough to class to make the distinction even meaningful. The result is simply a general vernacular. Coleridge also finds objectionable and impracticable Wordsworth's claim that there is no essential difference between the language of poetry and that of prose. Coleridge dissects a number of Wordsworth's poems. And Wordsworth was particularly sensitive to Coleridge's criticism; as Gill notes, Wordsworth dropped 'Alice Fell' from editions of his poetry after Coleridge's critique in chapter 18 of *Biographia Literaria*, only to restore it to his *Poetical Works* after Coleridge's death (*MW* 702). Having heard Wordsworth recite *The Prelude*, Coleridge knew that Wordsworth's great strength was writing in his own voice, in what he considered to be a philosophical mode, and disliked Wordsworth's 'predilection for the *dramatic* form in certain poems' (2: 135). But in the end Coleridge excuses the defects of Wordsworth's poetry because they are so closely related to the virtues of it—although discussion of those virtues takes place in considerably fewer pages than the censure does. In terms of the literary canon, Coleridge's assessment of Wordsworth has proven to be well-founded: 'in imaginative power, he stands nearest of all modern writers to Shakespear and Milton; and yet in a kind perfectly unborrowed and his own' (2: 151). Certainly, even as writers such as Dickens and Joyce may have superseded Wordsworth in popularity or as subjects of scholarly study, no *poet* would be able to stand so firmly with Shakespeare and Milton as Wordsworth came to in the two centuries following his great decade.

FOR FURTHER STUDY

1. Mary Robinson's collection *Lyrical Tales* appeared in 1800 just before the second edition of *Lyrical Ballads*. Although many of the individual poems were published in newspapers, some inspired by the first edition of *Lyrical Ballads*, Robinson's volume as a whole clearly stands as a response to Wordsworth and Coleridge. The original volume *Lyrical Tales* is available digitally via Google Books—what poems in it seem to respond to poems from *Lyrical Ballads*? How so?
2. How does Shelley's sonnet 'To Wordsworth' employ Wordsworth's 'Intimations Ode'?
3. On of the most indelible portraits of the collaboration appears in Hazlitt's essay 'My First Acquaintance with Poets' (1823). Hazlitt, upon visiting the trio of Wordsworth, Coleridge, and Dorothy Wordsworth, had free access to the *Lyrical Ballads*

poems in manuscript and enjoyed Coleridge's recitation of Wordsworth's 'Idiot Boy.' Here Hazlitt provides a crucial sense of how both poets read aloud their poetry—both in a manner like 'a chaunt' but Coleridge's recitation 'more full animated, and varied,' while Wordsworth's was 'more equable, sustained, and internal.' He goes on to describe Coleridge's reading 'dramatic' and Wordsworth's 'lyrical' (103–5). Read this widely reprinted essay and think of it in terms of Hazlitt's representation of the early collaboration so many years later. What does it tell us about the early days? What does it tell us about the poets' reputations in the 1820s and the early construction of Romanticism?

4. The most important chapter of *Biographia Literaria* for the study of Wordsworth and Coleridge's collaboration is chapter 14. Note that this chapter is the source of Coleridge's famous discussion of the 'willing suspension of disbelief' in relation to his part in the project. Read this chapter for the way it presents a slightly different take on the first edition than Wordsworth's Preface. How does Coleridge defend Wordsworth? How does Coleridge critique Wordsworth? In particular, compare Coleridge's description of a poet, 'in *ideal* perfection,' with Wordsworth's in the Preface.

5. Read Wordsworth's later poem 'Extempore Effusion upon the Death of James Hogg' (1835) for a view of Wordsworth's own sense of his outliving his contemporaries (*MW* 370).

CHAPTER 5

INFLUENCE AND INTERPRETATION

INFLUENCE

In 1841 Elizabeth Barrett called Wordsworth 'the king-poet of our times' (qtd. in Gill, *Victorians* 10). Her future husband, however, did not share her reverence. When Wordsworth accepted the laureateship in 1843, Robert Browning took it as the final compromise of the once-great liberal poet and spiritual leader: his poem on Wordsworth, 'The Lost Leader' (1845), recalls Shelley's sonnet 'To Wordsworth' from nearly 30 years before, opening with the image of Wordsworth as a new Judas: 'Just for a handful of silver he left us, / Just for a riband to stick in his coat.' Despite Browning's harsh assessment, the Victorian Wordsworth seemed to readers largely apolitical. And after his death—particularly in the eyes of 'Wordsworthians,' a quasi-religious group of Victorian followers—he had become a mystical priest of nature and a moral philosopher. His didactic tendencies suited the Victorians' taste for morally instructive and emotionally affecting literature. Upon Wordsworth's death, Matthew Arnold composed 'Memorial Verses' (1850) which allied him with two other poets—Goethe and Byron—whose presence persisted as part of the early Victorian consciousness, but whose influence Arnold predicts will fail to prove as inimitable as Wordsworth's:

> Ah! since dark days still bring to light
> Man's prudence and man's fiery might,
> Time may restore us in his course
> Goethe's sage mind and Byron's force;
> But where will Europe's latter hour
> Again find Wordsworth's healing power?
> Others will teach us how to dare,
> And against fear our breast to steal;
> Others will strengthen us to bear—
> But who, ah! who, will make us feel? (58–67)

Arnold's tribute elides more recent writers such as Tennyson and Dickens who were following in Wordsworth's footsteps. In particular, the popularity of Tennyson and his succession to the position of Poet Laureate confirms that the Victorians saw a natural progression from one poet to the next, and that Wordsworth had finally become part of the cultural fabric of the Victorian period to a considerably greater extent than he had been during his own 'great decade.' Similarly, in his *Autobiography*, John Stuart Mill writes of Wordsworth's poetry as 'medicine' for his depression, finding in his poems 'a source of inward joy, of sympathetic and imaginative pleasure, which could be shared in by all human beings' (121). Similarly, John Ruskin, comparing him with Coleridge, extolled Wordsworth in even more effusive terms:

> Wordsworth may be trusted as a guide in everything, he feels nothing but what we ought all to feel—what every mind in pure moral health *must* feel, he says nothing but what we all ought to believe—what all strong intellects *must* believe. (392)

These effects on Mill and Ruskin are as close as anyone could come to articulating the effect Wordsworth undoubtedly hoped to have on his readers. Such appreciation of Wordsworth gave him the aura of being both a poet and a philosopher—as the memorial tablet installed in Grasmere Church in 1851 identifies him. For many in the Victorian period Wordsworth was, in the words inscribed on that memorial, 'a chief minister, not only of noblest poesy, but of high and sacred truth.'

Wordsworth's importance for American writers was apparent at the same time. Selections from *Lyrical Ballads* began appearing in America in 1799 and became fairly popular, with a two-volume edition finally appearing in 1802. The American reception of Wordsworth largely was free of the kind of vitriol that fueled reviews by British critics such as Jeffrey. The most popular American poet of the nineteenth century, Henry Wadsworth Longfellow, was greatly influenced by Wordsworth's experiments in poetic diction and narrative, as a poem such as 'Paul Revere's Ride' (1860) demonstrates. Although probably more influenced intellectually by Coleridge than by Wordsworth, Ralph Waldo Emerson made the voyage and trek to meet Wordsworth in person at Rydal Mount in 1833; and he wrote an essay on Wordsworth for *The Dial* in 1843. Wordsworthian ideas pervade Emerson's *Nature* and Emerson's poetry; for example, the short lyric 'The Apology' (1846) seems practically a rewriting of 'Expostulation and Reply' and 'The Tables Turned.' Frequently ambivalent about the elder poet, Emerson could not deny Wordsworth's originality and his increasing sway on American culture. The thought of Wordsworth and Coleridge pervades American Transcendentalism, which is now commonly called American Romanticism. In addition to the connections between their ideas about Nature, Henry David Thoreau shows the influence of Wordsworth's insistence upon simpler language in both poetry and prose—although Thoreau famously quipped that, as a Nature poet, was not rough and ready enough for a country still in touch with its wilderness and its native inhabitants: 'Wordsworth is too tame for the Chippeway' (321). In general American intellectuals such as Emerson, Thoreau, and Bronson Alcott recognized affinities among Wordsworth's emphases on subjectivity, individualism, self-reliance, Nature, egalitarianism, and humanitarianism, and the ideals of what was still the American experiment and the philosophy of their Transcendental Club. Certainly Walt Whitman's *Leaves of Grass* (1855) has Wordsworthian strains—one American reviewer, comparing Whitman to Wordsworth, even wondered what Francis Jeffrey would have thought of it.

Wordsworth's reputation grew steadily in the nineteenth century. Thanks largely to the advice of Tennyson, Francis Palgrave included more poetry by Wordsworth than any other poet in his hugely influential *Golden Treasury of English Songs and Lyrics* (1861). Wordsworth's editor William Knight founded the Wordsworth Society in 1880, which included among its members Leslie Stephen and John Ruskin (Gill, *Victorians* 236). While declining to join the Society, Arnold as critic and editor contributed greatly to the elevation of Wordsworth by attempting to disperse the blind idolatry of the Wordsworthians. Arnold's Preface to his 1879 edition of Wordsworth called for a serious reappraisal of Wordsworth—'not in the spirit of a clique, but in the spirit of disinterested lovers of poetry' (xxv). Specifically, Arnold, who believed the longer poems *The Excursion* and *The Prelude* to be greatly flawed, asserted that Wordsworth's reputation could

never advance if he continued to be treated as a moral philo-
sopher—countering Leslie Stephen's treatment in his essay
'Wordsworth's Ethics' (1879). Similarly against such attempts at
philosophical systematizing, Walter Pater interpreted Wordsworth's
poetry purely for its aesthetics, reclaiming the poet's original
purpose of giving pleasure to the reader and showing that it was
possible to appreciate it without regard to philosophy, politics,
or biography. According to Pater, Wordsworth is 'the true fore-
runner of the deepest and most passionate poetry of our own
day' (63). Even Oscar Wilde, in the 1891 *The Decay of Lying*,
when considering Wordsworth as a poet rather than a Nature-
worshipper, is more generous than one might expect. Also in
1891, the Reverend Stopford Brooke founded the Wordsworth
Trust to preserve Dove Cottage, where Wordsworth lived for most
of 'the great decade.' The Wordsworth Trust continues to oper-
ate today in Grasmere, where visitors can tour Dove Cottage
and scholars can work in the museum, research centre, and read-
ing room. Indeed, the Wordsworth Trust is a major cultural
institution in Britain.

INTERPRETATION

The debate over Wordsworth as simple aesthete versus Wordsworth
as moral philosopher would continue in the twentieth century,
as important literary scholars such as A. C. Bradley would
oppose the aesthetic reading of Wordsworth by emphasizing yet
again the visionary qualities, while formalist 'New Critics' would
attempt to read the poetry strictly in terms of what the text says
about itself. But Wordsworth did not prove to be as adaptable to
New Critical close reading as some seemingly more difficult
poets would be. Modern critics and Modernist poets struggled
with Wordsworth's simplicity. The Victorian Wordsworth seemed
too, in Thomas Hardy's bitterly ironic words, 'breezy and pure'
for an increasingly violent and chaotic century (24). After World
War II, however, and upon the centenary of his death, scholars
and critics came to understand Wordsworth as a more compli-
cated poet. Lionel Trilling's groundbreaking essay 'Wordsworth
and the Iron Time' (1950) (later retitled 'Wordsworth and the
Rabbis'), in part a response to T. S. Eliot's disparagement of
Wordsworth in his *The Use of Poetry and the Use of Criticism*
(1933), explored the intellectually challenging and comparably

'Judaic' aspects of Wordsworth's mysticism and quietism—aspects that make him sadly incompatible with modern literature and modern life. Trilling thus issued a challenge to make Wordsworth relevant again. The work of M. H. Abrams and Harold Bloom did much to rehabilitate Romanticism against the assaults leveled on it by Modernism, not just in poetry but in practically all of the arts. In their own ways, Bloom and Abrams revived the view of Wordsworth as visionary, philosophical poet, as their critical readings and edited collections firmly upheld the canon of the 'Big Six' Romantic poets—Blake, Wordsworth, Coleridge, Byron, Shelley, Keats. In *The Ringers in the Tower* (1971), Bloom finds that 'modern poetry, in English, is the invention of Blake and Wordsworth' (17). Abrams' masterpiece, *Natural Supernaturalism* (1971), works from the basic premise that 'Wordsworth . . . was the great and exemplary poet of his age' (14). As it turns out, Bloom and Abrams, both great admirers and astute readers of Wordsworth, have had the most significant influence on the shaping of the canon of literature in English as it stands today.

By the 1970s Wordsworth's status in the literary canon was fixed, as Coleridge and Arnold had predicted, alongside Shakespeare and Milton (as far as poetry is concerned). In commemoration of Wordsworth's bicentenary in 1970, Wordsworth scholars and enthusiasts founded the scholarly journal *The Wordsworth Circle* under the steadfast editorship of Marilyn Gaull; established the Wordsworth-Coleridge Association, which currently boasts more than 2,500 members; and gathered for the first Wordsworth Summer Conference in Grasmere, where participants continue to meet annually for two weeks of poetry, papers, and fellwalking. Another major development in the 1970s was the emergence of the so-called Yale School of criticism, which included Bloom, Geoffrey Hartman, and Paul de Man, for whom Wordsworth became a major subject of study. These critics turned what seemed to the New Critics to be Romantic poetry's shortcomings—its apparent lack of a unified complexity—into what makes it interesting, focusing specifically on the indeterminacy of language and symbol. Almost a deconstructionist, Hartman in particular opened up new ways of reading Wordsworth without there having to be a false coherency. By focusing on this disparate complexity and inspiring considerable critical debate, they also helped to make *The Prelude* a more prominent work in Wordsworth's corpus than ever before. Hartman's seminal study *Wordsworth's Poetry, 1787–1814* (1964, reprinted 1971) complicates, without discarding, the interpretation of Wordsworth as visionary. Hartman's criticism—itself a kind of creative writing—presents a divided, confused, and irreconcilable self-consciousness in Wordsworth's poetry that creates provocative verbal gaps in meaning. Hartman's book set the stage for virtually every reading of Wordsworth that followed during the subsequent 20 years. Paul de Man, for instance, draws out the darker implications of this kind of extreme close reading, finding language frequently in conflict with meaning. De Man's approach is especially profound when he considers *The Prelude* in relation to the impossibility of actualizing the self—the enterprise of autobiography—within a system of language. This emphasis on language in Wordsworth was carried on by Frances Ferguson in her important book *Wordsworth: Language as Counter-Spirit*, which studies Wordsworth's awareness of language as a kind of existential crisis, and his resultant attempts to control the contingencies of language with his elaborate classification of his poems.

The installation of Wordsworth as the chief poet of the academic rubric 'the Romantic Period' was concomitant with the culmination of twentieth-century discussions of Romanticism and its limitations as a critical category. Historically minded scholars such as Marilyn Butler and Jerome McGann encouraged a rethinking of the concept of Romanticism as it had been defined around the middle of the century by critics Arthur O. Lovejoy and René Wellek and then reaffirmed by Bloom and Abrams. Even before then, the traditional definition of Romanticism had become oversimplified for the ease of instruction, classification, and periodization, presenting Wordsworth and Coleridge as radical innovators at odds with the 'neoclassicism' of the eighteenth century. After McGann's *The Romantic Ideology*, scholars could no longer ignore the fact that 'Romanticism' was practically an *ad hoc* Victorian-period construction that Abrams and others had reified in their critical work. Wordsworth and Coleridge never would have considered themselves to be 'Romantic,' and for the Victorians, the chief 'Romantic' writer would have been Sir Walter Scott. McGann and others recognized that the concept of Romanticism was an ahistorical aesthetic deduction that in practice had excluded many important writers from the period. Wordsworth and Byron at their best, for instance, could not be farther apart in style and interests; and yet a narrow definition of 'Romanticism' would seem to imply a similarity that is actually fallacious. Moreover, Wordsworth's ascendency made him a target for challenges to traditional Romanticism and the literary canon. In the 1980s and 1990s critics such as Marlon Ross, Anne Mellor, Mary Jacobus (*Romanticism*), and Judith Page interrogated the values implicit in the Romantic canon—and Wordsworth's place in it—from the point of view of feminism and gender studies, while politically oriented New Historicists such as Marjorie Levinson, James Chandler, David Simpson, and Alan Liu raised controversy and inspired new approaches by questioning Wordsworth's political and social commitments through their study of the poetry in terms of what it elides or obviates. These approaches in turn have been challenged by such scholars as Abrams ('On Political Readings'), Thomas McFarland, and Nicholas Roe. As Kenneth R. Johnston's *The Hidden Wordsworth* shows, there may still be much to learn about the poet's life and his activities. The historical Wordsworth and the poetry in its context continue to be the primary interest of scholars at the start of the twenty-first century.

WHICH WORDSWORTH?

Editors of the past 50 years or so have substantially reconstructed Wordsworth's literary career. The study of various published versions and manuscripts and stages of writing and revision has complicated the way we read Wordsworth's poetry and how we go about selecting which version to read. Although usually only scholars care about such matters, the reader of Wordsworth's poetry also can participate these days in questions about which version of a poem to read. Changes in editorial theory and practice have given us a particularly dynamic and various Wordsworth that accords well with what we might expect from an author whose career spans more than 50 years and multiple authoritative versions of his most famous poems from various stages of his career. Readers as well as editors now understand that the Wordsworth who collaborated with Coleridge on *Lyrical Ballads* is a very different poet from the one Queen Victoria appointed

Poet Laureate. This difference makes not only a biographical or historical point but also what scholars call a textual crux. Which Wordsworth, embodied in the various texts of his poems, do we want to read? It is a critical commonplace that Wordsworth's poetry after the so-called great decade of 1798–1807 is not as compelling—although, as we have seen, this was not the case for Victorian readers—so critics have come to question the value of reading revised versions of those poems from later in Wordsworth's career. In other words, if he did not write good poetry in his later years—and few readers today think that did— then why should we trust his poetic judgment when he then made changes to the poems that he wrote in his prime? The selection of text greatly affects reading and interpretation, which, in turn, influence our sense of the relevance of an author and ultimately the endurance of that author in the literary canon.

For most of the twentieth century, editorial policies have privileged the latest authorized version of a literary text, so most anthologies or editions have tended to reprint literary works in the form the author apparently wished for them to be read. Following this principle, the standard for most of the twentieth century was Ernest de Selincourt's five-volume edition, first published in 1941–1949 and then revised by Helen Darbishire in 1952–1959. Writers do give serious thought to their literary afterlife, hoping for and, in some cases, deliberately providing for poetic immortality. Although new challenges have emerged, this kind of editorial approach still survives—most predominantly for today's readers in the pages of *The Norton Anthology of English Literature*, where many of the fundamental textual issues regarding Wordsworth's poetry, and others' works, have played out since the early 1970s. Under the general editorship of M. H. Abrams, one of the most esteemed Romanticists, the *Norton Anthology* was for decades the leading (i.e., best-selling) anthology for British literature—seriously challenged only recently by the *Longman Anthology of British Literature*—and thus a kind of literary bible. Another important Romantic scholar and editor, Jack Stillinger, continues to oversee the Romantic-period section of the *Norton*. Here appeared the first canonical representation of Wordsworth's 'The Ruined Cottage' (see Chapter 3) based on Jonathan Wordsworth's 1969 edition. The inclusion of a work in the *Norton* means that it has, in a sense, arrived, having

been studied and debated by scholars and critics and its impor-
tance thus established by experts. But because the anthology
provides the foundation for the study of literature in colleges
and universities—most often in literature-survey courses—its
editorial principles have a great impact on the way instructors
and their students encounter writers and their work. It involves
more than quibbling over punctuation; and for Wordsworth,
the selection of a reading text requires that an editor must decide
which Wordsworth they want to represent.

The case of 'Simon Lee' provides an illustration of a textual
crux that even general readers ought to find interesting, for it
greatly involves them in the choice of which Wordsworth they
want to read. Wordsworth's revision of 'Simon Lee' for his 1832
Poetical Works makes the poem much more conventional: it
dispenses with some of the narrative innovation in the original's
wild shifts between past and present that we saw in Chapter 3.
We might even regard the later version as a different poem that
is both less challenging and more sentimental, thus possibly
more in keeping with popular contemporary tastes. This revision
reveals a Wordsworth less engaged with social issues of his day
and more interested in his place in literary tradition: a conspicu-
ous allusion to Milton's 'Lycidas' seems to redefine the poem as
a traditional pastoral elegy and thus place it in a higher literary
register than the original which had challenged the literary
expectations of his contemporary readers while at the same time
making a social point that to them would have seemed some-
what radical. The later version instead caters to a popular read-
ership and its conventional expectations by aligning Wordsworth
in a classical tradition that goes back to Virgil. But it is in fact
this later version of 'Simon Lee' that is reprinted in the *Norton
Anthology of English Literature*, although the composition and
publication dates indicated are 1798. While it is true that a ver-
sion of the poem called 'Simon Lee' appeared in print in 1798,
the unsuspecting reader will believe that the poem they are read-
ing is the poem that appeared in *Lyrical Ballads*. It is not.

Stillinger's decision to print the later version of 'Simon Lee' is
a matter of editorial principle. Other editors since the 1970s have
argued for printing the earliest complete versions of the poems,
even if those versions were never published. Stephen Parrish has

guided the production of the multivolume Cornell Wordsworth edition according to this principle: the individual volumes present reading texts that reflect the state of the poems in surviving manuscripts with notes that present changes in later versions. Stillinger, in objection to this practice, calls it 'textual primitivism' and has argued that readers should read the final version authorized by the poet, for it is these later versions that made Wordsworth's reputation. More recent interest in the historical moment of publication has shown a preference for reading the texts as they first appeared in print, without much regard for manuscript versions or later revisions. For example, the Gill edition that I have cited throughout sometimes presents less-familiar versions of poems, such as, for example, 'I Wandered Lonely as a Cloud' or 'Resolution and Independence,' because they were the original versions. Admittedly, this is the practice I have followed in my own editorial work and is the way I tend to present literature to students. But this approach is not unproblematic either because it may result in ignoring the poet's intentions altogether—and does occasionally pit an editor's aesthetic judgments against the author's. For instance, Jonathan Wordsworth once wrote that 'poets are known by the best versions of their works: Wordsworth is almost exclusively known by the worst' (xiii). While this approach still may allow for the comparison of all forms of the text, it does emphasize the study of literature in its historical, political, social, and literary contexts. Take, for example, the case of *Peter Bell*: Stephen Gill's edition for Oxford World's Classics presents the text from the manuscript version of 1798, showing the poem as Wordsworth originally conceived it and thus rightly as it appears in that particular stage of Wordsworth's poetic development. If the student of Romantic-period poetry is interested, say, in Percy Bysshe Shelley's parody of Wordsworth, *Peter Bell the Third*, he or she would find Gill's text unsatisfactory because Shelley was responding to the version of the poem Wordsworth finally published more than 20 years later. This student would want to read the 1819 published version of *Peter Bell*. A comparison of the 1798 manuscript version with Shelley's parody would be incongruous. The 1798 version, however, would be the more appropriate one to compare with other poems from *Lyrical Ballads*. So, thanks to the scholarly work of his various editors, we have access to many Wordsworths and may gain a sense of Wordsworth as he was writing, Wordsworth as he was read, and Wordsworth as he wanted to be read.

These textual issues are even more complicated when it comes to Wordsworth's *The Prelude*. This major work—for most readers today Wordsworth's masterpiece—has a complicated life-span from its 1798 inception in Germany to its 1850 publication by the poet's widow. If we attend to what we perceive to be an author's wishes, we might exclude this work altogether since Wordsworth himself never oversaw its publication. But that would be a tremendous loss because the poem, as we have seen, provides such insight into Wordsworth's greatest ideas and most exquisite poetry. But there are, as with 'Simon Lee,' multiple versions. If there is one more authoritative than another, it would have to be the 1850 *Prelude* presented posthumously to the public and reflecting the poet's final revisions. But if we are thinking of Wordsworth as the great poet of Romanticism, the author of the Preface to *Lyrical Ballads*, we must also consider the fact that the 1850 *Prelude* was published the same year as Tennyson's *In Memoriam*, Elizabeth Barrett Browning's *Sonnets from the Portuguese*, Hawthorne's *The Scarlet Letter*, and Dickens' *David Copperfield*. Does it become a different poem read alongside these other works? Readers might wish to consider *The Prelude* and *David Copperfield* together as 'portraits of the artist as a young man'—since David Copperfield the character is both a novelist and at least partly autobiographical. In this regard, too, *The Prelude* becomes chronologically and thematically contemporaneous with Browning's *Aurora Leigh*, a long blank-verse poem about the growth of a *woman* poet's mind published in 1856. Moreover, if we read the 1850 *Prelude* alongside *In Memoriam*, we find two poems with strikingly similar Christian perspectives that may seem incongruous with the poetry of the younger, more iconoclastic Wordsworth. This *Prelude*, therefore, ought to be considered a major text of the Victorian period; but because Wordsworth is known as the great Romantic poet, his work appears in anthologies grouped with writers two generations previous to the 'early' Victorian writers for whom his work would be so important. Wordsworth is not so much the iconic

Romantic but rather an iconoclast, whose career continues to influence poets into the twenty-first century.

FOR FURTHER STUDY

1. If Wordsworth's *The Prelude* is both Romantic and Victorian, how might we consider a writer such as Dickens Romantic? What Wordsworthian elements appear in a famously Dickensian work such as *A Christmas Carol*—particularly in the portrayal of Scrooge's childhood and of Tiny Tim and the Cratchit family? How might Scrooge's reformation involve Wordsworthian concepts?

2. What are the advantages and disadvantages of using the concept of 'Romanticism' to define a literary period? If we call the succeeding period 'the Victorian Period,' should we redefine literary periods for much of the eighteenth century according to the reigns of the Georges? Does it even make sense to define literary periods in terms of political epochs? Finally, should we return to the older term 'the Age of Wordsworth' to define this period?

3. In what ways are the following twentieth- and twenty-first-century writers poetic descendents of Wordsworth? Robert Frost (see 'The Oven Bird,' 'Birches,' 'Design'); W. B. Yeats ('The Wild Swans at Coole,' 'Among School Children'); Wallace Stevens ('The Idea of Order at Key West,' 'Of Mere Being'); Theodore Roethke ('Meditation at Oyster River,' 'Moss-Gathering'); Ted Hughes ('Relic,' 'Daffodils'); James Dickey ('The Heaven of Animals,' 'Trees and Cattle'); Seamus Heaney ('Digging,' 'The Skunk,' 'Blackberry-Picking'); Fleur Adcock ('Prelude'); Eavan Boland ('That the Science of Cartography Is Limited'); Louise Glück ('The Red Poppy'); Philip Levine ('A Walk with Tom Jefferson'); Dan Albergotti ('The Osprey and the Late Afternoon').

CHAPTER 6

GUIDE TO FURTHER READING

STANDARD EDITION OF WORDSWORTH'S POETRY

Parrish, Stephen, general ed. *The Cornell Wordsworth*. Ithaca: Cornell UP, 1975–2007. 21 vols.

SCHOLARLY JOURNAL

The Wordsworth Circle was founded in 1970 as a forum for scholarly work on the first generation Romantic-period writers, complementing the already established *Keats-Shelley Journal*. Founding editor Marilyn Gaull continues to direct the journal, which regularly features articles by the top scholars in Romantic studies, reviews of significant new books, and special issues on the most important issues and debates in the field. See, for example, special issues on Wordsworth's *Excursion* (9 [Spring 1978]), on teaching Wordsworth (9 [Autumn 1978]), on 'the Great *Prelude* Debate' (1805 vs. 1850) (17 [Winter 1986]), and on perhaps Wordsworth's greatest interpreter, Geoffrey Hartman (37 [Winter 2006]).

FURTHER READING AND STUDY

Critical commentary and scholarly research on Wordsworth is quite extensive. What follows is a select list of resources that I find useful and that I would recommend to the reader of this book as next steps in studying Wordsworth. It is not comprehensive, and I have omitted some particularly advanced or difficult works. Many of the resources below will direct interested readers to those and many other sources.

Since detailed commentary on Wordsworth's *The Prelude* is beyond the scope of this book, I encourage readers to consult the following resources for reading Wordsworth's masterpiece. Many of the subsequent sources listed in this chapter contain discussions of *The Prelude*; but for beginning study of the poem, the following are the best places to start. I list them in order of priority:

1. Wordsworth, William. *The Prelude: 1799, 1805, 1850.* Norton Critical Edition. Ed. Jonathan Wordsworth, M. H. Abrams, and Stephen Gill. New York: Norton, 1979.
2. Gill, Stephen. *William Wordsworth:* The Prelude. Landmarks of World Literature. Cambridge: Cambridge UP, 1991.
3. Johnston, Kenneth R. *Wordsworth and* The Recluse. New Haven: Yale UP, 1984.
4. Gill, Stephen, ed. *William Wordsworth's* The Prelude: *A Casebook.* Oxford: Oxford UP, 2006.
5. Onorato, Richard J. *The Character of the Poet: Wordsworth in* The Prelude. Princeton: Princeton UP, 1971.

Other Useful Introductions to Wordsworth

Abrams, M. H., ed. *Wordsworth: A Collection of Critical Essays.* Englewood Cliffs, NJ: Prentice-Hall, 1972.

Gill, Stephen, ed. *The Cambridge Companion to Wordsworth.* Cambridge: Cambridge UP, 2003.

Mahoney, John L. *William Wordsworth: A Poetic Life.* New York: Fordham UP, 1997.

Williams, John. *William Wordsworth.* Critical Issues. Houndmills, Basingstoke: Palgrave, 2002.

—. *William Wordsworth: A Literary Life.* New York: St. Martin's, 1996.

Woodring, Carl. *Wordsworth.* Boston: Houghton Mifflin, 1965.

Wordsworth, Jonathan, Michael C. Jaye, and Robert Woof. *William Wordsworth and the Age of English Romanticism.* New Brunswick: Rutgers UP, 1987.

Select Biographies

Barker, Juliet. *Wordsworth: A Life.* 2000. New York: HarperCollins, 2005.

Gill, Stephen. *William Wordsworth: A Life.* Oxford: Oxford UP, 1989.

Moorman, Mary. *William Wordsworth: A Biography; The Early Years, 1770–1803.* Oxford: Oxford UP, 1957.

—. *William Wordsworth: A Biography; The Later Years, 1803–1850.* Oxford: Oxford UP, 1965.

Wu, Duncan. *Wordsworth: An Inner Life.* 2002. Oxford: Blackwell, 2004.

Recommended Critical Books on Wordsworth's Poetry and Career

Averill, James H. *Wordsworth and the Poetry of Human Suffering.* Ithaca: Cornell UP, 1980.

Beer, John. *Wordsworth and the Human Heart.* New York: Columbia UP, 1978.

Ferguson, Frances. *Wordsworth: Language as Counter-Spirit*. New Haven: Yale UP, 1977.

Fry, Paul H. *Wordsworth and the Poetry of What We Are*. New Haven: Yale UP, 2008.

Galperin, William. *Revision and Authority in Wordsworth: The Interpretation of a Career*. Philadelphia: U of Pennsylvania P, 1989.

Gill, Stephen. *Wordsworth and the Victorians*. Oxford: Clarendon, 1998.

Gravil, Richard. *Wordsworth's Bardic Vocation, 1787–1842*. Basingstoke: Palgrave, 2003.

Hanley, Keith. *Wordsworth: A Poet's History*. Basingstoke: Palgrave, 2001.

Hartman, Geoffrey H. *Wordsworth's Poetry, 1787–1814*. 1964, 1971. Cambridge: Harvard UP, 1987.

Matlak, Richard E. *Deep Distresses: William Wordsworth, John Wordsworth, Sir George Beaumont, 1800–1808*. Newark: U of Delaware P, 2003.

McFarland, Thomas. *William Wordsworth: Intensity and Achievement*. Oxford: Clarendon, 1992.

Perkins, David. *Wordsworth and the Poetry of Sincerity*. Cambridge: Harvard UP, 1964.

Pirie, David B. *William Wordsworth: The Poetry of Grandeur and of Tenderness*. London: Methuen, 1982.

Sheats, Paul D. *The Making of Wordsworth's Poetry, 1785–1798*. Cambridge: Harvard UP, 1973.

Waldoff, Leon. *Wordsworth in His Major Lyrics*. Columbia: U of Missouri P, 2001.

Wordsworth, Jonathan. *William Wordsworth: The Borders of Vision*. Oxford: Clarendon, 1982.

Wordsworth and *Lyrical Ballads*

Bialostosky, Don H. *Making Tales: The Poetics of Wordsworth's Narrative Experiments*. Chicago: U of Chicago P, 1984.

Cronin, Richard, ed. *1798: The Year of the* Lyrical Ballads. New York: St. Martin's, 1998.

Gamer, Michael. *Romanticism and the Gothic: Genre, Reception, and Canon Formation*. Cambridge: Cambridge UP, 2000.

Glen, Heather. *Vision and Disenchantment: Blake's* Songs *and Wordsworth's* Lyrical Ballads. Cambridge: Cambridge UP, 1983.

Gravil, Richard. '*Lyrical Ballads* (1798): Wordsworth as Ironist.' *Critical Quarterly* 24.4 (1982): 39–57.

Jacobus, Mary. *Tradition and Experiment in Wordsworth's* Lyrical Ballads. Oxford: Clarendon, 1976.

Johnston, Kenneth R. 'The Triumphs of Failure: Wordsworth's *Lyrical Ballads* of 1798.' *The Age of William Wordsworth: Critical Essays on the Romantic Tradition*. Ed. Johnston and Gene W. Ruoff. New Brunswick: Rutgers UP, 1987. 133–59.

Jordan, John E. *Why the* Lyrical Ballads? *The Background, Writing, and Character of Wordsworth's 1798* Lyrical Ballads. Berkeley: U of California P, 1976.

Manning, Peter J. ' "Michael," Luke, and Wordsworth.' *Criticism* 19 (1977): 195–211.

—. 'Troubling the Borders: *Lyrical Ballads* 1798 and 1998.' *The Wordsworth Circle* 30 (1999): 22–7.

Mayo, Robert. 'The Contemporaneity of the Lyrical Ballads.' *PMLA* 69 (1954): 486–522.

McEathron, Scott. 'Wordsworth, *Lyrical Ballads,* and the Problem of Peasant Poetry.' *Nineteenth-Century Literature* 54 (1999): 1–26.

Parrish, Stephen Maxfield. *The Art of the* Lyrical Ballads. Cambridge: Harvard UP, 1973.

Trott, Nicola, and Seamus Perry, eds. *1800: The New* Lyrical Ballads. Basingstoke: Palgrave, 2001.

Wordsworth and Coleridge

Bialostosky, Don H. 'Coleridge's Interpretation of Wordsworth's Preface to *Lyrical Ballads.*' *PMLA* 93.5 (1978): 912–24.

Eilenberg, Susan. *Strange Power of Speech: Wordsworth, Coleridge, and Literary Possession.* New York: Oxford UP, 1992.

Gravil, Richard. 'Coleridge's Wordsworth.' *The Wordsworth Circle* 15.2 (1984): 38–46.

—. 'Coleridge and Wordsworth: Collaboration and Criticism from *Salisbury Plain* to *Aids to Reflection.*' *The Oxford Handbook of Samuel Taylor Coleridge.* Ed. Frederick Burwick. Oxford: Oxford UP, 2009. 24–48.

Hazlitt, William. 'My First Acquaintance with Poets.' 1823. *The Selected Writings of William Hazlitt.* Vol. 9. Ed. Duncan Wu. London: Pickering & Chatto, 1998. 95–109.

Magnuson, Paul. *Coleridge and Wordsworth: A Lyrical Dialogue.* Princeton: Princeton UP, 1988.

Matlak, Richard E. *The Poetry of Relationship: The Wordsworths and Coleridge, 1797–1800.* New York: St. Martin's, 1997.

McFarland, Thomas. *Romanticism and the Forms of Ruin: Wordsworth, Coleridge, and the Modalities of Fragmentation.* Princeton: Princeton UP, 1981.

McGann, Jerome J. 'The *Biographia Literaria* and the Contentions of English Romanticism.' *Coleridge's* Biographia Literaria: *Text and Meaning.* Ed. Frederick Burwick. Columbus: Ohio State UP, 1989. 233–54, 306–8.

Modiano, Raimonda. 'Coleridge and Milton: The Case against Wordsworth in the *Biographia Literaria.*' *Coleridge's* Biographia Literaria: *Text and Meaning.* Ed. Frederick Burwick. Columbus: Ohio State UP, 1989. 150–70, 286–90.

Newlyn, Lucy. *Coleridge, Wordsworth, and the Language of Allusion.* 1986. Oxford: Oxford UP, 2004.

Ruoff, Gene W. *Wordsworth and Coleridge: The Making of the Major Lyrics, 1802–1804*. New Brunswick: Rutgers UP, 1989.

Sisman, Adam. *The Friendship: Wordsworth and Coleridge*. New York: Viking, 2006.

Walker, Eric C. '*Biographia Literaria* and Wordsworth's Revisions.' *Studies in English Literature* 28 (1988): 569–88.

Wheeler, Kathleen M. *Sources, Processes and Methods in Coleridge's* Biographia Literaria. Cambridge: Cambridge UP, 1980.

Wordsworth and Romanticism

Abrams, M. H. *English Romantic Poets: Modern Essays in Criticism*. 2nd ed. Oxford: Oxford UP, 1975.

—. *Natural Supernaturalism: Tradition and Revolution in Romantic Literature*. New York: Norton, 1971.

Blank, G. Kim. *Wordsworth's Influence on Shelley: A Study of Poetic Authority*. New York: St. Martin's, 1988.

Bloom, Harold. *Romanticism and Consciousness: Essays in Criticism*. New York: Norton, 1970.

—, ed. *The Visionary Company: A Reading of English Romantic Poetry*. 2nd ed. Ithaca: Cornell UP, 1971.

Gaull, Marilyn. *English Romanticism: The Human Context*. New York: Norton, 1988.

Johnston, Kenneth R., and Gene W. Ruoff, eds. *The Age of William Wordsworth: Critical Essays on the Romantic Tradition*. New Brunswick: Rutgers UP, 1987.

—, et al., eds. *Romantic Revolutions: Criticism and Theory*. Bloomington: Indiana UP, 1990.

Manning, Peter J. *Reading Romantics: Text and Context*. Oxford: Oxford UP, 1990.

Newlyn, Lucy. *Reading, Writing, and Romanticism: The Anxiety of Reception*. Oxford: Oxford UP, 2003.

Rzepka, Charles J. *The Self as Mind: Vision and Identity in Wordsworth, Coleridge, and Keats*. Cambridge: Harvard UP, 1986.

Wolfson, Susan J. *The Questioning Presence: Wordsworth, Keats, and the Interrogative Mode in Romantic Poetry*. Ithaca: Cornell UP, 1986.

Wordsworth and Politics/History

Abrams, M. H. 'On Political Readings of *Lyrical Ballads*.' *Romantic Revolutions: Criticism and Theory*. Ed. Kenneth R. Johnston et al. Bloomington: Indiana UP, 1990. 320–49.

Benis, Toby R. *Romanticism on the Road: The Marginal Gains of Wordsworth's Homeless*. Basingstoke: Macmillan, 2000.

Bromwich, David. *Disowned by Memory: Wordsworth's Poetry of the 1790s*. Chicago: U of Chicago P, 1998.

Butler, Marilyn. *Romantics, Rebels and Reactionaries: English Literature and Its Background, 1760–1830*. Oxford: Oxford UP, 1981.

Chandler, James. *Wordsworth's Second Nature: A Study of the Poetry and Politics*. Chicago: U of Chicago P, 1984.

Friedman, Michael H. *The Making of a Tory Humanist: William Wordsworth and the Idea of Community*. New York: Columbia UP, 1979.

Harrison, Gary. *Wordsworth's Vagrant Muse: Poetry, Poverty and Power*. Detroit: Wayne State UP, 1994.

Johnston, Kenneth R. *The Hidden Wordsworth: Poet, Lover, Rebel, Spy*. New York: Norton, 1998.

Langan, Celeste. *Romantic Vagrancy: Wordsworth and the Simulation of Freedom*. Cambridge: Cambridge UP, 1995.

Levinson, Marjorie. *Wordsworth's Great Period Poems: Four Essays*. Cambridge: Cambridge UP, 1986.

—. 'Wordsworth's Intimations Ode: A Timely Utterance.' *Historical Studies and Literary Criticism*. Ed. Jerome J. McGann. Madison: U of Wisconsin P, 1985. 48–75.

Liu, Alan. *Wordsworth: The Sense of History*. Stanford: Stanford UP, 1989.

Pfau, Thomas. *Wordsworth's Profession: Form, Class, and the Logic of Early Romantic Cultural Production*. Stanford: Stanford UP, 1997.

Richey, William. 'The Politicized Landscape of "Tintern Abbey".' *Studies in Philology* 95 (1998): 197–219.

Rieder, John. *Wordsworth's Counterrevolutionary Turn: Community, Virtue, and Vision in the 1790s*. Newark: U of Delaware P, 1997.

Roe, Nicholas. *Wordsworth and Coleridge: The Radical Years*. Oxford: Clarendon, 1988.

Simpson, David. *Wordsworth's Historical Imagination: The Poetry of Displacement*. New York: Methuen, 1987.

Spargo, R. Clifton. 'Begging the Question of Responsibility: The Vagrant Poor in Wordsworth's "Beggars" and "Resolution and Independence".' *Studies in Romanticism* 39 (2000): 51–80.

Stafford, Fiona. 'Plain Living and Ungarnish'd Stories: Wordsworth and the Survival of Pastoral.' *Review of English Studies* ns 59 (2007): 118–33.

Williams, John. *Wordsworth: Romantic Poetry and Revolution Politics*. Manchester: Manchester UP, 1989.

Wordsworth and Nature (Landscape, Ecology, and Environmentalism)

Bate, Jonathan. *Romantic Ecology: Wordsworth and the Environmental Tradition*. London: Routledge, 1991.

Brennan, Matthew. *Wordsworth, Turner, and Romantic Landscape*. Columbia: Camden House, 1987.

Fulford, Tim. *Landscape, Liberty and Authority: Poetry, Criticism and Politics from Thomson to Wordsworth*. Cambridge: Cambridge UP, 1996.

Heffernan, James A. W. *The Re-Creation of Landscape: A Study of Wordsworth, Coleridge, Constable, and Turner*. Hanover: UP of New England, 1984.

Kroeber, Karl. *Romantic Landscape Vision: Constable and Wordsworth*. Madison: U of Wisconsin P, 1975.

McCracken, David. *Wordsworth and the Lake District: A Guide to the Poems and Their Places*. Oxford: Oxford UP, 1985.

McKusick, James C. *Green Writing: Romanticism and Ecology*. New York: St. Martin's, 2000.

Miall, David S. 'Locating Wordsworth: "Tintern Abbey" and the Community with Nature.' *Romanticism On the Net* 20 (November 2000). Web.

Oerlemans, Onno. *Romanticism and the Materiality of Nature*. Toronto: U of Toronto P, 2002.

Pite, Ralph. 'How Green Were the Romantics?' *Studies in Romanticism* 35.3 (1996): 357–73.

Roe, Nicholas. *The Politics of Nature: William Wordsworth and Some Contemporaries*. 2nd ed. Basingstoke: Palgrave, 2002.

Wesling, Donald. *Wordsworth and the Adequacy of Landscape*. London: Routledge, 1970.

Wordsworth and Gender/Women Writers

Cross, Ashley J. 'From *Lyrical Ballads* to *Lyrical Tales*: Mary Robinson's Reputation and the Problem of Literary Debt.' *Studies in Romanticism* 40 (2001): 571–605.

Fulford, Tim. *Romanticism and Masculinity: Gender, Politics, and Poetics in the Writings of Burke, Coleridge, Cobbett, Wordsworth, De Quincey, and Hazlitt*. Cambridge: Cambridge UP, 1999.

Jacobus, Mary. *Romanticism, Writing and Sexual Difference: Essays on* The Prelude. Oxford: Clarendon, 1989.

Labbe, Jacqueline M. 'Revisiting the Egotistical Sublime: Smith, Wordsworth, and the Romantic Dramatic Monologue.' *Fellow Romantics: Male and Female British Writers, 1790–1835*. Ed. Beth Lau. Farnham, Surrey: Ashgate, 2009. 17–38.

Page, Judith W. *Wordsworth and the Cultivation of Women*. Berkeley: U of California P, 1994.

Richey, William. 'The Rhetoric of Sympathy in Smith and Wordsworth.' *European Romantic Review* 13.4 (2002): 427–43.

Ross, Marlon B. *The Contours of Masculine Desire: Romanticism and the Rise of Women's Poetry*. New York: Oxford UP, 1989.

Ward, John Powell. ' "Will No One Tell Me What She Sings?": Women and Gender in the Poetry of William Wordsworth.' *Studies in Romanticism* 36 (1997): 611–33.

Watkins, Daniel P. *Sexual Power in British Romantic Poetry*. Gainesville: UP of Florida, 1996.

Wolfson, Susan J. '*Lyrical Ballads* and the Language of (Men) Feeling: Wordsworth Writing Women's Voices.' *Men Writing the Feminine: Literature, Theory, and the Question of Genders*. Ed. Thaïs E. Morgan. Albany: State U of New York P, 1994. 29–57.

Wordsworth and Dorothy Wordsworth

Fay, Elizabeth A. *Becoming Wordsworthian: A Performative Aesthetics.* Amherst: U of Massachusetts P, 1995.

Heinzelman, Kurt. 'The Cult of Domesticity: Dorothy and William Wordsworth at Grasmere.' *Romanticism and Feminism.* Ed. Anne K. Mellor. Bloomington: Indiana UP, 1988. 52–78.

Levin, Susan M. *Dorothy Wordsworth and Romanticism.* New Brunswick: Rutgers UP, 1987.

Mellor, Anne K. *Romanticism and Gender.* New York: Routledge, 1993.

Reiman, Donald H. 'Poetry of Familiarity: Wordsworth, Dorothy, and Mary Hutchinson.' *Romantic Texts and Contexts.* Columbia: U of Missouri P, 1987. 183–215.

Soderholm, James. 'Dorothy Wordsworth's Return to Tintern Abbey.' *New Literary History* 26 (1995): 309–22.

Thomson, Heidi. ' "We Are Two": The Address to Dorothy in "Tintern Abbey".' *Studies in Romanticism* 40 (2001): 531–46.

Wilson, Frances. *The Ballad of Dorothy Wordsworth.* New York: Farrar, 2008.

Wolfson, Susan J. 'Individual in Community: Dorothy Wordsworth in Conversation with William.' *Romanticism and Feminism.* Ed. Anne K. Mellor. Bloomington: Indiana UP, 1988. 139–66.

Woof, Pamela, ed. *The Grasmere and Alfoxden Journals.* By Dorothy Wordsworth. 2002. Oxford: Oxford UP, 2008.

Wordsworth and Philosophy

Bewell, Alan J. *Wordsworth and the Enlightenment: Nature, Man, and Society in the Experimental Poetry.* New Haven: Yale UP, 1989.

Durrant, Geoffrey. *Wordsworth and the Great System: A Study of Wordsworth's Poetic Universe.* Cambridge: Cambridge UP, 1970.

Hatherell, William. ' "Words and Things": Locke, Hartley, and the Associationist Context for the Preface to *Lyrical Ballads*.' *Romanticism* 12 (2006): 223–35.

Hirsch, E. D., Jr. *Wordsworth and Schelling.* New Haven: Yale UP, 1960.

Kelley, Theresa M. *Wordsworth's Revisionary Aesthetics.* Cambridge: Cambridge UP, 1988.

Simpson, David. *Wordsworth and the Figurings of the Real.* Atlantic Highlands: Humanities Press, 1982.

Wordsworth and Poetry/Poetic Form

Abrams, M. H. 'Structure and Style in the Greater Romantic Lyric.' *From Sensibility to Romanticism: Essays Presented to Frederick A. Pottle.* Ed. Frederick W. Hilles and Harold Bloom. 1965. London: Oxford UP, 1970. 527–60.

Behrendt, Stephen C. 'Placing the Places in Wordsworth's 1802 Sonnets.' *SEL: Studies in English Literature, 1500–1900* 35.4 (1995): 641–67.

Bennett, Andrew. *Wordsworth Writing.* Cambridge: Cambridge UP, 2007.

Burwick, Frederick. 'Wordsworth and the Sonnet Revival.' *Colloquium Helveticum* 25 (1997): 117–41.

Curran, Stuart. *Poetic Form and British Romanticism.* New York: Oxford UP, 1986.

—. 'Wordsworth and the Forms of Poetry.' *The Age of William Wordsworth: Critical Essays on the Romantic Tradition.* Ed. Kenneth R. Johnston and Gene W. Ruoff. New Brunswick: Rutgers UP, 1987. 115–32.

Curtis, Jared R. *Wordsworth's Experiments with Tradition: The Lyric Poems of 1802.* Ithaca: Cornell UP, 1971.

Harvey, G. M. 'The Design of Wordsworth's Sonnets.' *Ariel: A Review of International English Literature* 6 (1975): 78–90.

Johnson, Lee M. *Wordsworth and the Sonnet.* Copenhagen: Rosenkilde and Bagger, 1973.

Mazzaro, Jerome. 'Tapping God's Other Book: Wordsworth at Sonnets.' *Studies in Romanticism* 33 (1994): 337–54.

O'Donnell, Brennan. *The Passion of Meter: A Study of Wordsworth's Metrical Art.* Kent: Kent State UP, 1995.

Robinson, Daniel. ' "Still Glides the Stream": Form and Function in Wordsworth's *River Duddon* Sonnets.' *European Romantic Review* 13.3 (2002): 449–64.

Wolfson, Susan J. *Formal Charges: The Shaping of Poetry in British Romanticism.* Stanford: Stanford UP, 1997.

Zimmerman, Sarah M. *Romanticism, Lyricism, and History.* Albany: State U of New York P, 1999.

Wordsworth and America

Gravil, Richard. *Romantic Dialogues: Anglo-American Continuities, 1776–1862.* Basingstoke: Palgrave Macmillan, 2000.

Newton, Annabel. *Wordsworth in Early American Criticism.* 1928. Chicago: U of Chicago P, 1969.

Pace, Joel, and Matthew Scott, eds. *Wordsworth in American Literary Culture.* Basingstoke: Palgrave Macmillan, 2005.

Simpson, David. 'Wordsworth in America.' *The Age of William Wordsworth: Critical Essays on the Romantic Tradition.* Ed. Kenneth R. Johnston and Gene W. Ruoff. New Brunswick: Rutgers UP, 1987. 276–90.

WORKS CITED

Abrams, M. H. *The Mirror and the Lamp: Romantic Theory and the Critical Tradition.* 1953. London: Oxford UP, 1971.

—. *Natural Supernaturalism: Tradition and Revolution in Romantic Literature.* New York: Norton, 1971.

—. 'Structure and Style in the Greater Romantic Lyric.' *From Sensibility to Romanticism: Essays Presented to Frederick A. Pottle.* Ed. Frederick W. Hilles and Harold Bloom. 1965. London: Oxford UP, 1970. 527–60.

Arnold, Matthew. 'Memorial Verses.' *Matthew Arnold: The Oxford Authors.* Ed. Miriam Alott and Robert H. Super. Oxford: Oxford UP, 1986. 137–9.

—, ed. *Poems of Wordsworth.* 1879. London: Macmillan, 1882.

—. 'Wordsworth.' *Essays in Criticism: Second Series.* London: Macmillan, 1888. 122–62.

Bateson, F. W. *English Poetry: A Critical Introduction.* London: Longmans, 1950.

Bentley, G. E., Jr. *Blake Records.* Oxford: Oxford UP, 1969.

Bialostosky, Don H. *Making Tales: The Poetics of Wordsworth's Narrative Experiments.* Chicago: U of Chicago P, 1984.

Bloom, Harold. *Genius: A Mosaic of One Hundred Exemplary Creative Minds.* New York: Warner, 2002.

—. *The Ringers in the Tower: Studies in the Romantic Tradition.* Chicago: U of Chicago P, 1971.

—. *The Western Canon: The Books and Schools for the Ages.* New York: Harcourt Brace, 1994.

Brennan, Matthew C. 'Wordsworth's "I Wandered Lonely as a Cloud".' *The Explicator* 57.3 (1999): 40–3.

Brewer, William D. 'The Prefaces of Joanna Baillie and William Wordsworth.' *Friend: Comment on Romanticism* 1.2–3 (1991–1992): 34–47.

Brooks, Cleanth. 'Irony as a Principle of Structure.' 1951. Rpt. in *The Critical Tradition: Classic Texts and Contemporary Trends.* Ed. David H. Richter. Boston: Bedford, 1998. 757–65.

Browning, Robert. 'The Lost Leader.' 1845. *The Poems of Browning.* Ed. John Woolford and Daniel Karlin. Vol. 2. London: Longman, 1991. 177–9.

Byron, George Gordon. *Lord Byron: The Major Works.* Ed. Jerome J. McGann, Oxford UP, 2000.

Butler, James A. 'Poetry 1798–1807: *Lyrical Ballads* and *Poems, in Two Volumes.*' *The Cambridge Companion to Wordsworth.* Ed. Stephen Gill. Cambridge: Cambridge UP, 2003. 38–54.

Chandler, James. *Wordsworth's Second Nature: A Study of the Poetry and Politics*. Chicago: U of Chicago P, 1984.

Coleridge, Samuel Taylor. *Biographia Literaria; Biographical Sketches of My Literary Life and Opinions*. Ed. James Engell and W. Jackson Bate. Princeton: Princeton UP, 1983. 2 vols.

—. *Collected Letters of Samuel Taylor Coleridge*. Ed. Earl Leslie Griggs. Vols. 1–2. Oxford: Clarendon, 1956.

—. *Lectures 1809–1819: On Literature*. Ed. R. A. Foakes. Princeton: Princeton UP, 1987. 2 vols.

—. *Specimens of the Table Talk of the Late Samuel Taylor Coleridge*. London: John Murray, 1835. 2 vols.

Conran, Anthony E. M. 'The Dialectic of Experience: A Study of Wordsworth's "Resolution and Independence".' *PMLA* 75 (1960): 66–74.

Curran, Stuart. '*Multum in Parvo*: Wordsworth's *Poems, in Two Volumes* of 1807.' *Poems in Their Place: The Intertextuality and Order of Poetic Collections*. Ed. Neil Fraistat. Chapel Hill: U of North Carolina P, 1986. 234–53.

Curtis, Jared R. *Wordsworth's Experiments with Tradition: The Lyric Poems of 1802*. Ithaca: Cornell UP, 1971.

de Man, Paul. *The Rhetoric of Romanticism*. New York: Columbia UP, 1984.

Feldman, Paula R., ed. *British Women Poets of the Romantic Era, an Anthology*. Baltimore: Johns Hopkins UP, 1997.

Ferguson, Frances. *Wordsworth: Language as Counter-Spirit*. New Haven: Yale UP, 1977.

Gifford, William. *The Baviad: A Paraphrastic Imitation of the First Satire of Persius*. London: R. Faulder, 1791.

Gilchrist, Alexander. *Life of William Blake*. 1863. Vol. 1. Totowa: Rowman, 1973.

Gill, Stephen. *William Wordsworth: A Life*. Oxford: Oxford UP, 1989.

—. *Wordsworth and the Victorians*. Oxford: Clarendon, 1998.

—. 'Wordsworth's Poems: The Question of Text.' *Romantic Revisions*. Ed. Robert Brinkley and Keith Hanley. Cambridge: Cambridge University Press, 1992. 43–63.

Glen, Heather. *Vision & Disenchantment: Blake's* Songs & *Wordsworth's* Lyrical Ballads. Cambridge: Cambridge UP, 1983.

Godwin, William. *An Enquiry Concerning Political Justice, and Its Influence on General Virtue and Happiness*. London: G. G. J. and J. Robinson, 1793. 2 vols.

Hardy, Thomas. *Tess of the D'Urbervilles*. Ed. Tim Dolin. London: Penguin, 1998.

Hartman, Geoffrey H. *Wordsworth's Poetry 1787–1814*. 1964. New Haven: Yale UP, 1971.

Hazlitt, William. 'Mr Wordsworth.' *The Spirit of the Age*. 1825. *The Selected Writings of William Hazlitt*. Vol. 7. Ed. Duncan Wu. London: Pickering & Chatto, 1998. 161–9.

—. 'My First Acquaintance with Poets.' 1823. *The Selected Writings of William Hazlitt*. Vol. 9. Ed. Duncan Wu. London: Pickering & Chatto, 1998. 95–109.

Jacobus, Mary. *Romanticism, Writing and Sexual Difference: Essays on* The Prelude. Oxford: Clarendon, 1989.

—. *Tradition and Experiment in Wordsworth's* Lyrical Ballads. Oxford: Clarendon, 1976.

Johnston, Kenneth R. *The Hidden Wordsworth: Poet, Lover, Rebel, Spy*. New York: Norton, 1998.

—. *Wordsworth and* The Recluse. New Haven: Yale UP, 1984.

Keats, John. *Selected Letters of John Keats*. Ed. Grant F. Scott. Cambridge: Harvard UP, 2002.

Levinson, Marjorie. *Wordsworth's Great Period Poems: Four Essays*. Cambridge: Cambridge UP, 1986.

Liu, Alan. *Wordsworth: The Sense of History*. Stanford: Stanford UP, 1989.

Lovejoy, Arthur O. 'On the Discrimination of Romanticisms.' 1948. *English Romantic Poets: Modern Essays in Criticism*. Ed. M. H. Abrams. 2nd ed. London: Oxford UP, 1975.

Magnuson, Paul. *Coleridge and Wordsworth: A Lyrical Dialogue*. Princeton: Princeton UP, 1988.

Manning, Peter J. 'Wordsworth's Intimations Ode and Its Epigraphs.' *Journal of English and Germanic Philology* 82.4 (1983): 526–40.

Marsh, Florence G. 'Wordsworth's Ode: Obstinate Questionings.' *Studies in Romanticism* 5 (1966): 219–30.

Matlak, Richard E. *The Poetry of Relationship: The Wordsworths and Coleridge, 1797–1800*. New York: St. Martin's Press, 1997.

Mayo, Robert. 'The Contemporaneity of the Lyrical Ballads.' *PMLA* 69 (1954): 486–522.

McFarland, Thomas. 'The Symbiosis of Coleridge and Wordsworth.' *Studies in Romanticism* 11 (1972): 263–303.

—. *William Wordsworth: Intensity and Achievement*. Oxford: Clarendon, 1992.

Medwin, Thomas. *Conversations of Lord Byron*. 2nd ed. London: Henry Colburn, 1824.

Mellor, Anne K. *Romanticism and Gender*. New York: Routledge, 1993.

Mill, John Stuart. *Autobiography*. Ed. John M. Robson. London: Penguin, 1989.

Milton, John. *The Complete Poetry and Essential Prose of John Milton*. Ed. William Kerrigan, John Rumrich, and Stephen M. Fallon. New York: Modern Library, 2007.

Moore, Thomas. *The Journal of Thomas Moore*. Vol. 1. Ed. Wilfred S. Dowden. Newark: U of Delaware P, 1983.

Moorman, Mary. *William Wordsworth: A Biography; The Early Years 1770–1803*. Oxford: Clarendon, 1957.

Newlyn, Lucy. *Coleridge, Wordsworth, and the Language of Allusion*. 1986. Oxford: Oxford UP, 2004.

Page, Judith W. *Wordsworth and the Cultivation of Women*. Berkeley: U of California P, 1994.

Parrish, Stephen Maxfield. *The Art of the* Lyrical Ballads. Cambridge: Harvard UP, 1973.

—. '"The Thorn": Wordsworth's Dramatic Monologue.' *ELH* 24 (1957): 153–63.

Pater, Walter. *Appreciations, with an Essay on Style*. London: Macmillan, 1889.

Perkins, David. *Wordsworth and the Poetry of Sincerity*. Cambridge: Harvard UP, 1964.

Pope, Alexander. *Complete Poetical Works*. Ed. Herbert Davis. Oxford: Oxford UP, 1966.

Rev. of *Leaves of Grass*. *The Daily National Intelligencer* 14 (July 14, 1860). The Walt Whitman Archive. Web.

Rieder, John. *Wordsworth's Counterrevolutionary Turn: Community, Virtue, and Vision in the 1790s*. Newark: U of Delaware P, 1997.

Robinson, Daniel. '*Elegiac Sonnets*: Charlotte Smith's Formal Paradoxy.' *Papers on Language and Literature* 39.2 (2003): 185–220.

Roe, Nicholas. *The Politics of Nature: William Wordsworth and Some Contemporaries*. 2nd ed. Basingstoke: Palgrave, 2002.

Ross, Marlon B. *The Contours of Masculine Desire: Romanticism and the Rise of Women's Poetry*. New York: Oxford UP, 1989.

Ruoff, Gene W. *Wordsworth and Coleridge: The Making of the Major Lyrics, 1802–1804*. New Brunswick: Rutgers UP, 1989.

Ruskin, John. 'To the Rev. W. L. Brown.' *The Works of John Ruskin*. Vol. 4. Ed. E. T. Cook and Alexander Wedderburn. London: George Allen, 1903. 390–3.

Sheats, Paul D. *The Making of Wordsworth's Poetry 1785–1798*. Cambridge: Harvard UP, 1973.

Shelley, Mary. *The Journals of Mary Shelley, 1814–1844*. Ed. Paula R. Feldman and Diana Scott-Kilvert. Baltimore: Johns Hopkins UP, 1995.

—. 'Note on Peter Bell the Third, by Mrs. Shelley.' *The Complete Poetical Works of Percy Bysshe Shelley*. Ed. Thomas Hutchinson. London: Oxford UP, 1923. 357–8.

Simpson, David. *Wordsworth's Historical Imagination: The Poetry of Displacement*. New York: Methuen, 1987.

Stempel, Daniel. 'Revelation on Mount Snowdon: Wordsworth, Coleridge, and the Fichtean Imagination.' *Journal of Aesthetics and Art Criticism* 29 (1971): 371–84.

Stillinger, Jack. 'Textual Primitivism and the Editing of Wordsworth.' *Studies in Romanticism* 28 (1989): 3–28.

Taylor, Anya. 'Religious Readings of the Immortality Ode.' *Studies in English Literature, 1500–1900* 26 (1986): 633–54.

Thoreau, Henry David. *Journal*. Vol. 1. Ed. Elizabeth Hall Witherell et al. Princeton: Princeton UP, 1981.

Trilling, Lionel. 'The Immortality Ode.' *English Romantic Poets: Modern Essays in Criticism*. Ed. M. H. Abrams. London: Oxford UP, 1975. 149–69.

—. 'Wordsworth and the Iron Time.' *Kenyon Review* 12 (1950): 477–97.

Trott, Nicola. 'Wordsworth's Loves of the Plants.' *1800: The New Lyrical Ballads*. Ed. Trott and Seamus Perry. Basingstoke: Palgrave, 2001. 141–68.

Wellek, René. 'The Concept of "Romanticism" in Literary History.' *Comparative Literature* 1 (1949): 1–23, 147–72.

Wolfson, Susan J. *The Questioning Presence: Wordsworth, Keats, and the Interrogative Mode in Romantic Poetry*. Ithaca: Cornell UP, 1986.

Woodring, Carl. *Wordsworth*. Boston: Houghton Mifflin, 1965.

Woof, Robert. *William Wordsworth: The Critical Heritage*. Vol. 1. London: Routledge, 2001.

Wordsworth, Dorothy. *The Grasmere and Alfoxden Journals*. Ed. Pamela Woof. Oxford: Oxford UP, 2008.

Wordsworth, Jonathan. *The Music of Humanity: A Critical Study of Wordsworth's 'Ruined Cottage.'* London: Nelson, 1969.

Wordsworth, William. *The Excursion, Being a Portion of the Recluse, a Poem*. London: Longman, 1814.

—. *The Fenwick Notes of William Wordsworth*. Ed. Jared Curtis. London: Bristol Classical, 1993.

—. *The Letters of William and Dorothy Wordsworth: The Early Years*. 2nd ed. Ed. Ernest de Selincourt and Chester L. Shaver. Oxford: Clarendon, 1967.

—. *The Letters of William and Dorothy Wordsworth: The Later Years*. 2nd ed. Ed. Alan G. Hill and Ernest de Selincourt. Oxford: Clarendon, 1978–1988. 4 parts.

—. *The Letters of William and Dorothy Wordsworth: The Middle Years*. 2nd ed. Ed. Ernest de Selincourt, Mary Moorman, and Alan G. Hill. Oxford: Clarendon, 1969–1970. 2 parts.

—. *The Prose Works of William Wordsworth*. Ed. W. J. B. Owen and Jane Worthington Smyser. Oxford: Clarendon, 1974. 3 vols.

—. *The River Duddon, a Series of Sonnets: Vaudracour and Julia: And Other Poems. To which is Annexed, a Topographical Description of the Country of the Lakes, in the North of England*. London: Longman, 1820.

Yudin, Mary F. 'Joanna Baillie's Introductory Discourse as a Precursor to Wordsworth's Preface to *Lyrical Ballads*.' *Compar(a)ison* 1 (1994): 101–11.

INDEX